TESTAMENT

TESTAMENT

A POEM BY

G.C. WALDREP

AMERICAN POETS CONTINUUM SERIES, No. 149

BOA Editions, Ltd. ❖ Rochester, NY ❖ 2015

First Edition
15 16 17 18 7 6 5 4 3 2 1

For information about permission to reuse any material from this book please contact The
Permissions Company at www.permissionscompany.com or e-mail permdude@eclipse.net.

Publications by BOA Editions, Ltd.—a not-for-profit corporation
under section 501 (c) (3) of the United States Internal Revenue
Code—are made possible with funds from a variety of sources,
including public funds from the New York State Council on the
Arts, a state agency; the Literature Program of the National En-
dowment for the Arts; the County of Monroe, NY; the Lannan
Foundation for support of the Lannan Translations Selection Se-
ries; the Mary S. Mulligan Charitable Trust; the Rochester Area
Community Foundation; the Arts & Cultural Council for Great-
er Rochester; the Steeple-Jack Fund; the Ames-Amzalak Memo-
rial Trust in memory of Henry Ames, Semon Amzalak and Dan Amzalak; and contributions
from many individuals nationwide. See Colophon on page 154 for special individual acknowl-
edgments.

ART WORKS.
arts.gov

State of the Arts

NYSCA

Cover Design: Sandy Knight
Interior Design and Composition: Richard Foerster
Manufacturing: Versa Press, Inc.
BOA Logo: Mirko

Library of Congress Cataloging-in-Publication Data

Waldrep, George Calvin, 1968–
[Poems. Selections]
Testament : a poem / by G.C. Waldrep. — First edition.
    pages ; cm. — (American poets continuum series ; no. 149)
ISBN 978-1-938160-63-9 (softcover) — ISBN 978-1-938160-64-6 (ebook)
I. Title.
PS3623.A358A6 2015
811'.6—dc23

2014039941

BOA Editions, Ltd.
250 North Goodman Street, Suite 306
Rochester, NY 14607
www.boaeditions.org
A. Poulin, Jr., Founder (1938–1996)

TESTAMENT

Hawthornden Castle
6–29 July 2009

PART I
THE IMAGINED PLASTICITY OF THE VISIBLE

The body as sculpture. (Pageant, labyrinth.)
Wrapped like Central Park or Marin
in Christo's silk, wiving into a future
of minerals and taffeta, hypocausts and gorse.
We have computers to calculate the rocket's
rate of descent, its pure metaphor.

Everything's a ruin, you said, at least
in embryo, by which you meant possibility
as seduced or displaced by time.
We were not talking about the body
and our kitchen was a delirious semblance
of all our commensal desires.

We weren't talking about burying
your father, my father, anyone really.

Predicate: the mask with its fleshy
retinue, adrift over the fields
like so many mathematical kites.
Of course they're burning, I say, turning
away from the window. What?
you counter. The fields, or the kites?

❖

Aerial archaeology, cropmarks and hut rings,
ditches, enclosures—we place
our fingers in the grooved photograph and
the mind says *Almost,* the mind says
It is pleasurable to know where men have been.

Sleeping in the grooves at night,
faint musk of earth-nitre and defenses the mind
conceives, conjures, concedes to agriculture
and topography.
We sleep in the X-chromosome, the Y
keeps right on dreaming. Absent the body
it dreams another body, and another, man
into bull, bull into kestrel.

We are guests moving around inside a film
the dead are showing. Sure, you said.

I mistook you for a film, for a body in a film,
I said, when I woke up. Sure, you said
again, standing in our beautiful kitchen, sipping coffee,
crowded in among the animals and glass.

❖

Porter's seat's small theater
of foxglove and rust. I almost wrote "trust,"
as in vowel, something even mortal
pain and grief believe in.
Along with the best gods, all the other gods.

When they tell you
"Step into the light," it is not automatically
a sign you should step
into anything. Light. Language. Faith. History.

We study architecture
because we want to believe the material world
is more literate than this one,
the council estates with their tiny shops and cottages
and the great houses
slope-farmed into children preparing
for some future bewilderment, or something

more than "future," involving glass and more styptic
chemicals. A rushing wind, renewable.

❖

Dried husk of an abandoned station—
see, you can tell by the steps
leading up to what would have been
the platform, now vanished in a tangle of fox-

glove and some other flower I can't name.

Language is no stop to the body.
Language is a choice, a bargain the body
enters into. In this not unlike sex.
Body chaining into body, generative, generational.

If we like the same things are we then
sculpted   by that liking, that likeness.

❖

A choice: the castle, the chapel,
or else the exploded gunpowder manufactory.
(It's not much of a choice, you complain.)

It's not that we wander about
looking for the pastoral. The pastoral wanders
about looking for us. Without us
the pastoral is nothing: metamorphic occlusions,
some "digestive and genital organs of plants."

The sleeves of the cities suffer us.
The plackets of the countryside, the little farms:
they suffer us, buried
under this incredible weight of nitrogen
and the vapors nitrogen dandles.

Certain software can reproduce these and other
patterns. Some of them we call joy.

And you say, I am affected
by the verticality of it. You say, I am
afraid of falling, and, Would you terribly mind
switching places?

Now there are two of us.
As in the definition of that word, "liberal."
To give, vs. to be the recipient of a gift.
Which is the less terrible opponent
is not a question that makes sense, in the city.

❖

The moral imagination, you said.
It's like some sort of kitchen gossip, isn't it,
only nobody knows which kitchen she's in.
Predicate, not to build but
to have built. So pretty, this little Latin
in its porcelain dressing gown.
Blink once for yes, blink twice for no.

Predicate, to have lasted long, or not so long;
to have lasted this long. Sustained
but in the legal sense, meaning
You are right, but only in this moment.

Small children "make poison"
from the most colorful, most disgusting ingredients
they can lay their hands on
(overlay of Grimm or Disney as appropriate).
Then they wonder what to do with it.

Part of the pageant takes place
in the labyrinth, yes. The light is better there.

❖

I said, One of my few natural virtues
is loyalty. —Meaning you're trustworthy,
you elaborated. Which caught me off guard:
History is an exercise in narrative,
in distinguishing between loyalty and trust.

What we liked best
about the gunpowder manufactory
was the enormous waterworks—dams, gates,
sluices—that survived, in part,
because they lay below the surface
of the explosion.

There were railings, to restrain the animals.
I thought, what soothing sounds
some of the animals are making
to some of the other animals. I thought,
Predicate: to have made,
to have chosen the right sound.

What enormous meals they must have eaten,
you said, another way of looking
at the same problem. What you fear most
has already happened
and subject to gravity, like a wine glass
at a party. Because they were like us. Because
we could see their faces in the water.

❖

It is not, or not only, a function
of History (Faith. Language. Light).
We step into the dark, cramped
shop where the Bangladeshi woman
sells stationery, and we find it charming
but we don't say so, not there, not then.

What you considered a lie
I imagined as misplaced geography, an accident
of mapping or of maps. GIVE WAY vs. YIELD.

Heartbeats wrapped in cloth, in milk.
How can we sell them
is what language is asking itself, and
isn't the dystopia trying to utter something
beautiful and new,
bride material, honey-dusted?

Vestige, pronounced to rhyme with
Prestige, a brand of automobile nobody's
thought to market yet
in this particular dialect, this alphabet.

When Queen Victoria visited the caves
they were said to have been hung in red velvet.

Predicate: to have hung, to have been hung,
to have visited, to have been visited.
To market, to pronounce, to have pronounced.
Perfect: *per-fecto,* to have been
completed, to have been *made-through.*

There is no mention of this event in her diary.

❖

A bridal texture, something suffering wears
when capitalism calls gender out
and says "Hey, let's go grab some dinner."
You can record this in language or
you can ignore it without benefit
of language, without resorting to language.
Capitalism swaggers
outside language in the chrome shadow of

something like an enormous, gleaming motorcycle
we aren't sufficiently afraid of. Not yet.

The body makes a living and we don't
understand enough about particle physics
to come up with some alternative
preregistration algorithm for everyone
we've invited to the charrette
so far. The finches, the barberry bushes,
the silica, the honey locusts,
the geodes encrusted with amethyst are all
somehow outside the body's plans,
its careful calculations.

Ventriloquy: at once hygienic and parturitive.
Myth closes one door and opens three others
without telling you anything
useful about what's beyond the lintels.
You think you can see some lights moving
through one, but really you're not sure.

You could stay here, the body suggests, sensibly.
But myth shakes one of its heavy heads.

Why does it always feel like gender was a house
you set fire to, in childhood perhaps,
only you don't remember doing it, just some people
who told you the story later, claiming it was true?

❖

The greater horror: speech is, after all,
redundant, that is, mimetic. I keep confusing
the words for "money" and "world"
in various languages,
starting with the German. *Geld* vs. *Welt.*

There must be a rib for this, the silence
keeps breathing in mankind's
general direction. Take it out, take it out.

Your fortune, your lucky number,
LEARN TO SPEAK CHINESE.
Such a wealth of information,
we could have
made a gun from it, little fire-tongue
of intent vs. humiliation.

When I was eight a cousin
took me to a rough rock-and-roll concert
and left me there. A big man
with dilated eyes and a broken beer bottle
in one hand tried to edge past me
in the risers, fell heavily, cut my forearm.

No one has to "believe" in light.
It comes, as they say, with the territory.

◈

It is not about love. —That might help,
though, you tell me.
I mean, if it were about love.

Correction: it has always been about love.

Little sand patterns, a jet passes overhead
and a dog barks.
The way you smuggle some words in.
I mean, ultimately they're all
proper nouns, aren't they? The symbol
remembers when it slept inside the symbol.
This is no longer only a matter
of language, of libraries, ingress and egress.

Or we were stones attracting other
stones. Out there among the animals.

See, their beautiful faces.
How they crush and crumble in our hands.

❖

Waves of sound, images
of explosions, ripe fruit and pornography
are streaming through our bodies
right now, at dizzying speeds. Surely something
in each cell registers these frequencies

and dies a little, soldiers
unable to parse the slick surfaces
of vein and rut, lip and teeth.
It's not magic to say *I love you*
like Roman Catholicism loves the Monroe
Doctrine. It's not even alchemy.

Because one thing does not become
another thing. Because nobody is interfering
with all the little hats music wears.

You want one of those little hats
for yourself, don't you, the dystopia
whispers, wearing its "silence" mask.
(See, there we are on television.)

It would be better, you said,
if we had a dog—any large dog—with us,
here in the castle. And we could pet it,
and sleep with it, and take it
for long walks,
when we wanted to. —If we wanted to.

◈

We eat the ripe cherries from the arbor
and they are ripe, but also quite sour, so we talk
about what we could make with them
if we were far away, i.e. at home: pie, strudel.

In some versions the angel
placed at the eastern gate
bears a flaming sword. In some versions
not. Or she's still there
but has lost the sword, pawned it, lent it out
in what she claims was an act of mercy.

In some versions it was all a trick
of geography, that is, of the light, of mapping.
A translation meant for the other animals.

But I slept so deeply that night, you said.
I mean, it was less rest than a perfect *idea*
of rest: somebody else's idea, a Platonic rest,
something I read about in a book.

◈

First you make the tools
out of nothing. And from the tools,
you must make nothing. Then, out of nothing,
you must remake the tools.

Somebody asks me
whether I keep a garden at home.
I lie and say I do. I have no idea why I'm lying.

I like any story with nasturtiums in it
is one way to put it, this truth about lying, this tool.
Making a movie is another way to put it.
If you have enough light. If you can pay for it.

Little interruptions in the light
is how the plants see us.
Minuscule ghost-explosions, combustible.

◆

The city presents light as an interruption of light
which is why we go there.
And for the food, and for the cooing of pigeons
which reminds us what it would be like
to be wingèd after all, i.e. Icarus
was not the scared, ambitious boy we like to think
but rather some ancient concinnity,
a bit of skin caught in the projector, electric.

Season of mothers, season of Destroyers
and of the seas that bear them.
Is it any wonder, you say, and
I don't know what you mean but I
say Yes, meaning the sea is a superior fidelity.
It has a shape, it has a motion.

Predicate: to have possessed shape, suffered
motion. The big gods and the little gods,
the ones we stroke, and sleep with, and take long walks
with. The ones that lead us into
and then back out of the castle,
that little bit we can see *from* the castle
that is not in fact the castle.

We write this down, and suppose something
by it, place it above
the desk, the bed, the sideboard
with its diminutive constellations of glass.
We think glass is another word for it
because glass is breakable and we can see through it.

I think, It is not that much like a movie,
after all. You add, It depends on which movie,
which curative herb we are talking about.

Digitalis. Abbreviate poison for the human heart.

❖

My tongue, an ignorance. Little orchard
of brute senses. Starlings
fly through it and no, they are not like
the mind, mind's hand grasping and ungrasping, rather
an artist's conception of graphite
as a gas, something that expands to fill
any available volume.
(Light. Language. Faith. History.)

Half-dark the river, unchained from its mills,
how it pools and creels, pools and creels.
A scribble in a notebook from
what some dogs were doing, further along.
The songmark of orioles,
papermill phantom-whisper by the car park.

Now please read aloud from the strip of paper
you are still holding in your left hand.

Did I say strip of paper. I meant wedding garment.

There are leaves that recall the shapes
of human hands, tropism of some dynastic
paradiso. Just the same
we shave them from the land,
suits of clothes we never bothered trying on.

❖

A trick of oxygen, this snuffing of candles
with one's bare fingertips.
We believe what the scientists tell us
about the members of our bodies, their elemental
faiths, and then we use them.

Maxwell's Demon, sorting hydrogen from
oxygen without benefit of clergy.

The traditional arguments about sound
moving *through* matter, hammer/anvil/stirrup.
Objects, things that can be seen
in their daily offices, tasted, touched, handled.

In a separate development,
a visiting Egyptian novelist explains
that the reason there are no good
Egyptian restaurants in New York City
is the peculiar Egyptian genius
for failing (or refusing) to self-promote.

It wasn't as if anyone had lost anything,
any prophesied savior failed to show.
We were just trying it out, test-driving our notions
about mimesis and what it might mean.

It made pretty colors in the leaves and we
squandered them, and then we called that *snow.*

❖

Viral, this severance.
As if all the planes had returned safely
from the mission except one
and we were waiting for it,
half-angry and half-terrified and trying hard
to talk about something else.

Ivy-leafed toadflax embroidering
a crown on the lip of an ancient well.
Is it art(ful) to see it this way.

We made such beautiful use of Latin
in place of the willow groves,
the high places. We were waiting, but
not with that look you keep giving me.

Because if we don't, the crops will fail.
Because if we don't, this time
the magician really will saw the girl in half.

War was a story
somebody was telling, and then
we were in it, I mean, we found words for it.
Abracadabra. Presto change-o.

❖

Hotels built especially for constellations.
That is what he said, and lived as if it were so.

Yes, he sometimes baked the wood
in a kitchen oven,
in his mother's kitchen oven, so that
it would achieve a certain texture, so that
it would look or feel a certain way.

Contemporaneously I quit speaking
for the second time in my life.
I cut up ripe summer peaches and threw them
away, over and over again,
bowl after immaculate bowl.

Breviary vs. aviary: who would win?

God-spiral of plot, makeshift genuflection.

❖

Or: consider the exquisite geometry
of the calfskin glove.
You want it to stand outside History, but
somehow it keeps obtruding
into the story, a magic lantern
not meant for us. FIVE CENTS, PLEASE.

We want to touch without touching.
St. Icarus, restore a semblance.

What passed from hand to machine, and
back to hand; there was no
duplicity. (Invisible hand, invisible glove.)

And we were there, and talking it over
with the future, which seemed sincerely
interested, asking only
about the orphans, those other ones,
what would we do with them,
where would we find the proper clothing.

Restore *to* semblance. A minor
emendation, as tangency for intersection.

When you kneel into the hoarfrost,
even accidentally, your knees come up
wet. Your body's heat does this much
on its own. For a little while.

May I introduce you to my topological
anomaly, which I call *house.* And

we broke it, and out of it, and called that *pain.*

❖

If invisible hand, then invisible glove.
If invisible gym, then invisible
weights, the body's capacity
for leverage. The cone of night spindling
inland, this far north of the equator.

It is always just a little bit about dying.
The buckles and stays. The flight-pressed estuary.

This is where gender comes in,
embroidered wedding tent set up
on the president's lawn. Children use it
as their freedom, a video installation
without the capacity to offend
the ex-lover whose blithe envoi
we have now translated
into however many languages.

This isn't one of those languages, you noted.

What is it then. A little bit of wind
in the projector's mouth. Let yourself go
bankrupt, it's easy, all you do

is pour your soul into as many
different bottles
as you can collect, and package what's left over
as that mystery novel you're always
threatening to write, and which you will never
otherwise complete, so that's OK.

We can walk there, we can have a picnic.

Because film is already dead
when it comes to us, when we view the images
light produces, extruded through the corpse.

At the prom we had no time to test
whether all bodies fall at the same rate of speed,
so instead there was a lot of
drunkenness and dancing, and trying to figure out
which parked car was yours
vs. somebody else's. Various urban legends accrued.

We were aware of memory as it evolved
from experience, even *before*
it evolved from experience. Pentecostal, precogniscient.
There are only eight conic sections, after all.
Something *eros* has to deal with.

My student wrote, A snake understands
a child bent low over his blocks
because a snake unhinges its jaw in order to eat.
I disagreed, so she took that
part out. Which ruined the poem.

I lay in the back, in the bed of a friend's pickup
and watched the stars do their thing.
We did not assist in the investigation
of the theft. We did not assign pronouns.
We kept tripping over this enormous
sword one of us was carrying, as if it were on fire,
only nobody knew what fire was, yet.

The bunnies in the courtyards fled from us
in the direction of mathematics
and illness, the two things we hadn't yet sold.
We didn't have questions about
what made them human, and heterosexual.

We were still looking for evidence of the flood.

❖

Later, many monographs on Bonnard
and some stencils we kept dubbing.
A mannerist ecology, Lisa Robertson proclaimed,
and we believed her, in spite of

what the painters were declaring, namely
that realist figuration was somehow
coming back
and would be responsible for
health care and pigeons and bombs falling
and looking up into the mouth of an exorbitant
wheeling paradigm of native architecture
we remembered neither
demanding nor building with our bare hands.

And we want to keep it this way,
we all agreed, as a province
of gender, plangiform, ambiplexured.

There is nothing so immediate
as the human wrist.
It keeps happening, as if it's the history
not only of your body
but of all the other bodies your body
could be, or was, or could have been.

Predicate: all the bodies your body
could be, was, could have been.
"I heard." "I saw." Domestic interior
of the universal, the sea your stoup, your iron rail.
As if in fidelity to subjectivity
some—if not *election*, then release.

It's you and me and all this *city*, separated
by a bridge with some carved figureheads on it

and a body stashed inside.
—Guess which body, History murmurs.

❖

The flare of a match is produced
by the rapid oxidation of its chemical
outer coating, its pericarp
and we know we have to do something
quickly, communicate the process to some
other medium, some uninvited guest.

It is evening, approaching midnight.
The monuments of the city
kneel before the traffic the city wakes,
or seems to wake, from the shorn pavements.
If something goes wrong—terribly
wrong—we send out images
of the terrible wrongness, little flashes
of we-don't-know-what, not-really,
only how it behaves when we
express it as from a god's jug of milk.

The body as a museum for light.
It is not a book, it does not exist
in four dimensions the way a book does.
Time scars it in its cradling anger
and teaches us new textile protocols.

We bring candies to the patients
in the hospital, even though
they are too unwell to enjoy them.

The debate over whether light
is a form of fire, or fire a form of light,
goes on and on
and bores History so much it resurrects

Midas, in the form of a small
planet we live on.
Watch us move so carefully.

❖

In the museum, we encountered
a pair of human forms, anatomically correct,
sculpted entirely from telephone wire,
red yellow pink green and blue.
Slightly larger than life-size, which somehow
made us even more uncomfortable

but not uncomfortable in the way painting does
which makes us want to invoke
the Greeks, let the dog
back into the castle, into our beds.

This time, the surprise
was that the medicine actually *worked*.
We were able to see the city from inside
the city. And not just because of the fires,
though we saw them too,
jute music boxes someone left open too long.
Part of the history of the body
is that we used to own it.

Together we formed small companies.
Together we consumed the fruits of others' labor.

As if something rode in on that, and we were
burdens, or beasts. Little shoe-shaped
absences where the bullets caught
some clothes we happened to be wearing.
How heavy these feel, you said. I said, Sure.

❖

How to tell a remnant from a ruin,
for example. Built on absence
as residence, permitted by updraft and the kindness
of certain fungi, certain spores:
NO STOPPING OR STANDING HERE.

I release you, says the estuary.
I release you, says the moon, recombinant.
I mean, if you want them to. Tithe
and not-tithe, un-tithe
of strut from aperture. Your rosary—
I almost wrote bursary, suspended purse.

The body only meets us halfway.
What you are saying is that painting
was simply *Not Serious.* Ever.

and that inside painting a little man sits,
and he keeps the mechanism going, and we watch
and we gasp in wonder
as if it were something almost alive.

❖

It was spring, and my friend asked me
(and others) over to his farm for a work frolic.
He wanted to tear down an old shed in his pasture.
It had been well-built, this shed. He should have
put a new roof on it and left it
where it was. It took us the better part of the day
to clean it out and remove as much tin
and other metal from the exterior as we could.

Fine, he said. We'll just set fire to the rest.

Night was coming on. We doused the posts,
the beams and rafters in gasoline. Most were pine
and there was still a lot of loose straw inside,
a wealth of fluent surfaces. (See: TINDER.)

Growing up against the rear of the shed, so close
to the shed that nobody had ever much tried
to chop it down, was a wild cherry.
After the fire got going, somebody pointed out
that the tree was going to burn, too.

That was, my friend said slowly,
regrettable,   but unavoidable.

We went inside and sang hymns for a time,
then went back outside, after the sun had set
and the shed fire was at its zenith.
The cherry tree, being alive—full of spring sap—
took some time to catch. When it did,
it burned like a torch, with an audible *whoosh*.

I'm showing you this film inside the film
the dead are showing, which is about gender,
I think, I mean from what I've seen so far.
That's me, leaning against the pasture fence
at dusk, of course with my back to the camera.

—The branches, my friend said, suddenly,
pointing. They look like hair, don't they.
They look like human hair that's burning.

PART II
NOTES FROM A CITY SILENCE FLED

The poem as a disused work, an abditory.
Things hidden in plain sight.
The miners all work for the council now.

Getting inside the vibration
from which all matter depends:
as if work were an illness
from which art recovers, a long convalescence.
Or: as if art *were* the work, or the convalescence
outside of which matter lingers,
doubtful. We take its temperature.
We congratulate ourselves:
this mathematical problem, this persona.

Either you stretch forth your hand
to reach inside the black box, or else you do not.
All those voices coming from inside,
from the bottom of the sea.
Only some of them are human, and
we efface what we know, what they knew
in what we term their "last moments."

Predicate: dependent upon copula.
To prick, assent, affirm, decide.

The evacuated airport. The money shot.
You cannot get "too close"
to a decision of this magnitude, someone said, and
It becomes a part of you, the *you* in question.

❖

Narcissus to Echo to Shakespeare, foliate
astrogony. Something warms
inside the human body and we want to call it
by its first name, its original name.
Instead we listen to music.
We pass our children through the fire.

The curve of the plastic spoon
was so sharp I kept cutting the inside
of my mouth every time I took a bite
of my banana split, only
the cold so numbed the pain, I didn't know
how wounded I was (until later).

Illness kicks a stone through an imaginary
opening in two-dimensional space,
which it calls *the soul.*
The space, the stone, the opening.

Ventriloquy / gender / nation / asylum.

I had forgotten what it was like
to watch a bee creep inside the velvet
calyx of a flower, any flower
(bluebells, in this instance)—to disappear
momentarily into that sweetness. Only
I had not realized I'd forgotten.

❖

We ask our children what it's like
to pass through the fire, on one leg or three.
Patrimony as a vertical motion,
something the whole body must make
out of mammals, from the flayed
skins of mammals.
Decaffeinated by order of the state.

This is not that part of the pageant,
fear's Dopplered groove
and the business of fear, that is, biology.

When the car pulled up behind me
I expected a slur, or a threat. Or a shot.
I thought, I have money in two currencies
from two different continents
in my wallet. I thought, my wallet is
"genuine calfskin," meaning:
more skins, more flayed mammals.
I thought, minor characters
are constantly being dispatched and
carried out of the narrative by other
minor characters and this

is the basis of the abiding, urgent appeal
of the sentence as a grammatical form.

❖

From the peeling sill, the castle's brief
phantasm: now a hand's confringing breadth,
ecliptic, now horizon. Another movie.

What we wanted: to write, yes, but
with our bodies, like the bees or maybe frost.
Hence cutlery and parchment, vellum.

You write as if gender were one of many things
that had surprised you: private property;
an otter;   —a sudden primrose; capitalism
decked out in its nautical throes.

The copula again, as a shorthand for hope, i.e.
stay tuned, dear friends, there's more to come.
On its own, intransitive, we reserve

for aseity and its agents, the God or gods
we hang from hooks
in the kitchen. A god is not "to decide"
but "to have made a decision:" *Per-fecto*,
done, over and out, another argument
for photography, not so much bride as bridalness,
bridefulness: the act of briding, adducent.

❖

The body has no choice in this matter of
"belief." It is always observant.

In the castle, tea at 4, drinks at 6:30.
Fictions in a series, no I do *not* think it would be
a good idea
to "start over" with the purely
material because this would mean reinstating
weapons to their autobiographical places,
also the formal postures of 18th-century painting
by which we were taught not to see.

The note pinned carefully to the branch
is not for you. Even so, you remove it, unfold it.
The page is blank.

Incarnation as genre, astricted
in that same way. You cannot carry your wheat
to any other mill. The bones of egress
permit "sensual communication,"
another series of vibrations, only more slowly.

❖

Emended trinity: eye, bee, flower.
Now you see it, now you don't. Or: a unity,
effective momentary symbiosis.

Replace soundtrack with color wheel.
Blanchot: "Dying is the indiscretion wherein God,
become somehow and necessarily
a god without truth, surrenders to passivity."

The real has many faces, and we stand
for a long time, trying to pick out the perp
from the lineup, the accuser from the accused.

To what extent is geography
itself a lie: Where I am, where "I" is
not, some story sleep was telling and then
the Pakistani sprinter passes you
on the council-built rail path
for the second time, the third, the fourth.

Predicate: to record this motion.
To have so recorded. Word as object, planet,
distal summoning. Rosebank at duskfall:
something *in* it. Something *from* it. Geometry
vs. geophagy, the eye rotating
against its field of vision, its embroidered vest.

❖

Or an argument about surveillance
becomes entangled with Science, by which I mean
the confusion of science with choice.
Faith watches, faith listens
without which certain antique terms, "mercy"
and "charity," become mere glyphs, pictographs,
pop music anomalies from Sweden—
faintly ridiculous, how quaint the natives were.

Look, you say, the policemen on television
are dancing. And I look, but now
there's a cartoon of two dogs chasing one another.

I am no longer certain whether the hunger I feel
is my own, or someone else's.

Empty handbag left in the lavatory
sending out truce signals. Is mimetic, then, but
not a code one can punch
into the keypad by the castle gate.

Language, then, being a plea
for scale, for proportion. The city
suffers us, and we sleep
beneath its leather awning, in our bespoke clothes.

❖

Dearest labia, little death habits, the cosmos
whirs along in its delicate tracery and we
are the hair it's shedding. Is one more way
to put it, you argue. I don't disagree.

I couldn't find the light switch
in the library. Rather than ask, I decided
only to read books in daylight:
compendiums of architecture, of the language
of architecture which is really
just biography in more perdurable form.
Incise the letters, filigree
as appropriate. The sun is so lonely here.

Predicate: to have known
where you were going, coldwater flats
in republican guise. Nazi graffiti in the crotch
of an elm or what looks like an elm.
Sometimes you strike the rock
in the wrong moment, or in the wrong way,
or while saying the wrong words, and this
is the result: deciduous papermill
over which language keeps flowing.

We want to know we know
that others have known more (than we do).
We write stories about this, read them
at altitudes of 37,000 feet.
These are the untranslatable stories,
the Egyptian novelist assures us.
They read the same in every language.
What everybody wants is to see the movie.

❖

Embrace vs. *black box*: obscure marketing
soliloquies in the vicinity of Bronze
Age earthworks. I hear the engine and look up,
but not in the same way as before.

If you unlatch a gate, relatch it immediately:
rule #1 of country walking.
Territory vs. responsibility, I SPY.
A brief history of the countryside:
We need sheep! (no) *more* sheep, (no) *different*
sheep, (no) more of the *same* sheep (Dolly).

Step into the light, we whisper
to the ancestors, presumably wrapped in pelts,
only they don't hear us, or if they do
they don't believe heat has anything to say
the body doesn't already understand.

The animal research institute quit cloning sheep
or at least quit talking about it.

The King of Terrors imports maize to Britain
centuries ahead of Thanksgiving
and we call it *Mystery*, Satan bound for 10,000 years
in rope, upside down. It's a good story,
so we set fire to it. Then we move the stone.

❖

Song not corpse, but a body
without agency, a ventriloquist's dummy
(insert obligatory Templar reference
here). Whether your tongue
is bloody or bloodless is your affair.

Through the trademarked glass
of the conspiracy: more labyrinth,
more Latin, more synthetic
plasma donors. More re-enactors in woad,
murmuring into their cell phones.

We sit in the large chair
thinking has vacated, stretch our arms
and legs. Such intimate clockwork.

You want to know what
the government is going to do
with the money you are paying in taxes,
you say. After all,
there's a war on. —Spend it, I reply.

❖

At some point we wash language
carefully, dress it up
and place it in a box. Then we can call it
Faith. (History. Light. Action.)
It speaks to us the way objects speak to us,
through shape, form, function.
Are you writing this all down, you ask.

Death is observable, except for the moment
in which the observer blinks.

Inside this moment a little more death
is waiting, as if for a cue.

It was high summer. I tell my students
corpses lay so long on the fields
around Gettysburg, after the battle,
that bees nested in them,
in their wounds and (especially) their lungs.

If I consider war an artifact
I can pick it up, then put it down again.
What does this do to the hands?
It renders the hands bloodless, i.e. song.

❖

The skin is a conspiracy to keep the artifact
from breaking up, a language
of adhesion. Sound waves emerge from it
as light strikes, as the light
from the projector shines through.
Pretty little movie, this backyard barbecue.

In another dream, somebody I knew
(but had not seen in years) was all over the news
because she had developed a periodic
table for suffering.
All I remember is that it was very beautiful
and I wanted a copy, but when I rushed
up to her, after the press conference, she insisted
she didn't know me, had never known me.

There are many resurrections, the guidebook
explains. Perhaps this one is yours.

❖

The body retreats from the song
of the body. We study the other animals.

The sheep are stupid and dirty
and covetous and dull. They believe they have
two skins, one of which isn't
memory, and that this serves them well.
This is why sheep are never lonely
and why their bodies make
such beautiful science, such beautiful art.

The Victorians had this much
correct, our sustained anxieties about how
the past keeps measuring us
against the scale language proffers.

Aluminum, brushed steel, silk fabrics
in the pastel registers: suspension
of feeling *qua* feeling,
language withheld by order of the council.
Another painting, another Platonic rest.

❖

It makes some difference
whether this Icarus was a boy or a man.
It makes some difference whether
what we are really talking about is love.

SpellCheck refuses to recognize "Icarus"
as a noun. As verb, then?
As a rib, hooked into some flying buttress?

There were poems in the aftermath,
yes. (History. Light. Wood. Poison.)
As for the moral imagination
see it flickering over the great

Mary, the wooden Marys, the calcareous
Marys, the vegetable Marys in their
earthen casques, the chitinous
Marys in their leathery, translucent shells.

I want to see the policemen
dancing, I want to see the men
in their white masks
(the white men in their masks).
After the hurricane. Spliced into the film.
In the Mardi Gras parade.

"Here are the sirens of not knowing
everything," Carla Harryman writes.
Graves as earth-bullets.
We walk through them. Is it enough
that we walk through them, and don't know
it, and in our not-knowing, know.

❖

In the pageant, everybody is white.
Even actors who are not "white"
play as if they were, some in whiteface,
some finding other, less obvious ways
to model "whiteness."
It's a morgue emblem, money guesses.

Somebody makes your clothes, and
is it better to know who that person *is,*
or not? Children don't request
specific sculptures in the sculpture park.
They haven't grown that rib yet.

Because of blood clots in my lungs,
they sent me home with a 5-inch
gash in my abdomen.

At first a nurse came every day
to clean the wound, which wasn't
healing (by design). Later,
I had to clean it myself. I also had to
give myself shots in the stomach,
twice a day. —Music says:

Set the audience to work tailoring
some new idea about
jurisprudence and the happy endurance
of brand names beyond culture,
in the memory of culture.
Then cut it into the wet plaster
of the basement walls, to remind us
of what we thought we were building,
before all that money ran out.

❖

Genetics professes to show
not only how many of your Y-chromosome
ancestors are still dictating
the terms of your particular whiteness,
but also whether
you suffered the body in precisely
that way, as a stressor, a notational system.

The shots caused bruising, caused
the muscles and flesh of my stomach
to become knotted, gnarled,
hard, discolored little marbles of flesh
that seemed more active than my illness,
than any figure I had for illness.

A woman films herself
standing outside a wind tunnel
while explaining how wind tunnels work.

She's lost her luggage, yes, but not
the ignition of consciousness
affixed to vapor, provection
of self into grass, spade, antimony.

DEAD SLOW read the road signs
near the animal research facility.
Predicate: missing rib as skeleton key.
(Something is on fire
inside your camera, I think.)

Predicate: to find or base (anything)
upon the stated facts or conditions.
Which are: paper, ink,
event, volition, and, by 1868, the carrying
of the final letter of a given word
into the voicing of the succeeding word.

❖

Archive as prayer. The brain bathing
in its sweet serum, dreaming of dictators
it can address love letters to.
How many lives does gender have?

I mean, even their *dogs* smelled white,
you insisted, and I believed you, because
the toughs also all had dogs, they
were out walking their dogs, would a man
walking his dog mug another man?
With or without a dog? With
or without another man watching?

Railways wake up into nonexistence and
give us tests we fail.
All this egg strata, I thought
I heard you murmur in your sleep.

Is it any wonder physics keeps
the physical world
under surveillance at all times?

The riddle of the Green Man
in Rosslyn Chapel is that he's
a substitute, a joker, randomly replacing
other sigils, emblems, images
throughout the filigree. Trick or treat:
You're still human! I'm not.

❖

Eye, bee, flower: trinity of mistaken
identities, the eye buzzing
around the svelte body of the bee,
bee around the lush orgasm of the eye
the flower wants to possess.
The end of nationalism is in sight.

In childhood, everything was either a test
or a pattern. Earliest memories:
light through crib bars;
watching a train; riding another, different
train; cousin, sister, dog, cat.

Other children played doctor.
I played barber. I told the neighborhood
kids that if they didn't let me
cut their hair, the birds would have
nothing with which to build their winter
nests. These birds would die.
In the deep cold their bodies would plummet
to the ground, little feathered bombs.
I remember the last girl
to resist this narrative, the way I finally
coaxed her into my "barber's chair,"
the tears in her eyes. I shaved her bald.

Velvet ropes in drugstores on Sundays.
What you want to buy
vs. what you can't. Or is it the rope
itself you want, otherworldly
calligraphy, event horizon, your
dancing policemen, your border posse.

❖

Another memory: being taught
that a flag that has accidentally been allowed
to touch the ground must be burned
and then, after having accidentally
dropped a flag, while on flag duty before school,
trying to burn that flag, quickly.

Either something that was supposed to happen
would not happen, now, or else
something had already happened and
the preceding events were a falsehood, a lie.

Have you discussed this with your mother
asks the doctor/your father/your lover/that poet.
You shake the doll again and again,
hoping it will say something
else. Its plastic eyes flutter epileptically.

Predicate: the lie made perfect,
hidden in plain sight. Index finger, rib,
this bit of holy wood.

There are lines you can't see in the wind,
lines meteorologists reproduce.
This confuses and angers you.
You decide to think of the wind as God's clone,
genetically identical but pre-aged.

❖

It is not a question of genre.
The animals gathered by accident in the clearing
in the beam of the automatic camera.

Blame is organized thinking, to blame
is to organize the objects of thought
into constituencies. It is an electoral operation.
In America, presidential elections
are all, and essentially, about blame, about
who built the railroads and who is unbuilding
the essential truths, about Judaism
and progress, T-bills and global warming.

Practicing foreign languages is one way
of disguising one's identity as a voter.
Requesting a record of one's vaccinations,
going or not going to jail.

I have quit talking to you, you see.
Who is listening / not listening
is what the poem wants to know, and in this way
viviparous. Phantom limb syndrome:
How many lives does gender have?

The brain thinks you are whole,
and it tells you—the part of you that is "you"—
that you're hurting, even when you're not.
So you find a way to tell the brain
that yes, you *were* hurting, only it's "better now"
and then it will be, the experts assure us.

❖

Something moved is another way
of reminding yourself that yet another species

has gone extinct. While I type this.
While you read it. Give the box to Susan Sontag,
wait twenty years. Ask for it back.

Some of our burdens are for children.
Or, our children's children.
A manuscript, a king, a severed head.

At an early age some grasp
their power to instill fear in others.
(You're talking about yourself, you say.)
Red earth belongs to the devil:
scratch it and you'll die.
That cloud formation means a tornado
is coming our way, now we're all
going to die. (We *are* all going to die.)

Memory vs. shadow, concept vs. need.
We select a guest from the Book of Guests.
Deep in the earth lies something
we don't want anymore, or not enough,
not enough to build houses for it.

The notes to the performance
are perfectly clear:
We are not to stand up while the actors
are away from the stage, changing costume,
sipping coffee. We are to remain
in our seats, rigid, at attention, quite still.

❖

Faith as time's marionette, as a more
trustworthy advertisement for sleep.

(Neurology: *Geld* vs. *Welt*.
The sour cherries in the courtyard,

a crossing and recrossing
by virtue of the senses and, yes, choice.
There is never only *one* transgression,
one tensile strength.)

Are you acting like a victim, you ask
(I am asking).
—What does a victim act like?

Skilled in needletrades we bind
wounds until we hum *orchard, orchard.*
Put your tongue
into the song of it, why don't you.
You flying thing, you prince of the air.

This is a problem: money
only pretends to believe. We stand
outside, in the cold, watching
the puppets abuse one another, listening
to their epithets, their howls.

❖

Swoon, then, as a foreign language
we don't get older while practicing
because the body views *swoon*
as a singularity. Silence flees the city
swoon occupies, garments
sulfurous, phosphorescent in moonlight.

Pit of a cherry, pit of the stomach.
Clothes harden on the body
like papier mâché, something chewed
and broken. If we bend closer
we can still read the news crawl.

I don't buy into this idea of ethnic
homelands, you said. I shrugged.
Resisting the draft is good
for the complexion and also
the vocal cords, a form justice takes
in moments of excavated will.

Statistics as a kind of follow-up
yoga. Let me get lost in your chi-square,
honey. Yes, I watched the video.
No, I did not dream about the video.
I didn't have to dream about the video:
I kept reliving it in waking life.

❖

You will know the mammals
by their dancing, Spinoza said, and
the many colors of their hair.

Also, we like to wear masks.

One of the best pageants
was Middle English, only we forgot
the combination, the *open sesame.*
Whereas before, merely a door-
cast space. Magritte-like.
We can't see what's on the other side
vs. there is no "other side."

In the park, we all agreed
to let go of our balloons
at the same time. We even counted
(to three, of course). I say
you released your balloons early.
You said yours caught
the breeze first, flew higher.

Hunger ticks, like a watch.
Clay pipe, soap bubble. We tap
on the glass but nobody seems
to hear. No one lets us out.

If we put on the right mask,
we can't even *see* the glass.
Language is helpful in this way.

❖

We can tell a copy from the original
by its integument, its patina. Spectroscopy
becomes one of the more generous arts,
a domestic accommodation
(Light. Wood. Poison. Anima).

History is not like jewelry, you can't
wear it, I protested.
You shrugged. Threading an oak leaf
into a typewriter, castle-issue.

Ductless eyework in the masonry
perpendicular to the heart. *I wish,*
someone keeps repeating. The ladies
of the DAR, corseted, borne through
the city on their velveteen phaetons.

Gender acquires a rib and wears it
proudly. Patron to the higher orders,
into the moneyworld Persephone rejected
as a consolation prize for myth.

Step into the painting, art whispers.
The moral imagination
grinds its axe, sharpens its accordion.

❖

But then you wake up, and you're holding
not a gun in your hand, after all:
something else. Accordion, femur, credit
card. Some trademarked journalism.

It is very quiet in the forest,
in this clearing just inside the forest.
You were meeting someone
here—isn't that how the dream went?

The composer told me.
When you try to whistle, you make an ugly noise,
like a hawk that's just sighted prey.

You brush the insects from your hair.
This can be a little unnerving
because some of them breathe fire.
Your hair wields them like swords.

❖

Language is already skepticism,
Levinas maintains. Blanchot again:
"Writing, without placing itself
above art, supposes that one not prefer art,
but efface art as writing effaces itself."

For there are structures of power
that defy capitalism's monopoly
on all the major modern utilities,
gas, electricity, public transit.
For there are structures of power
that reinforce capitalism's monopoly
on all the major cultural
algorithms: painting, sculpture,
music, dance. Photography, film.

We live inside the noise photography makes.
Like birds in Central Park
we've learned to make the same noise,
both to one another
and when nobody else is around.

We dust the economy for latents.
This is not science. It is detection, an art.
A little math, a little chemistry
with a story inside. Something large and real
and beyond all sacrifice.

You were wrong about power, is what
the noise keeps saying. You were
wrong, wrong, wrong, wrong, wrong.

This is not cynicism. It is triage.
The media broadcast the chapter headings,
first in black and white, then in color.

❖

Things one forgets: the physical sensation
of pain. First love. The external
structures in which certain rooms were situated.
Things one never forgets: the international
telephone call you arrived too late to answer
(never to discover who called, or why).
The image of your sister entering the house
laughing, missing her footing on her first step
and shattering her teeth on the slate hearth.

Because things could have been different,
that's why. Pain = inevitability.
Structure is archetype, i.e. we live with it.

A constant murmuration of event,
prognostifying. Dowse with skeleton key
from behind this curtain wall
of (Faith. Light. Substance. Mystery).

To write in bad faith: after the fact.
(Predicate: *to record*, vs.
to have recorded.) The body as copula
when faced with copula: copula to copula.
The mirror, shattered, renews itself.
"The body wants to be art and fails at it."
Error is what sets the body free.

❖

In the winnowing chamber,
I find myself using a rib as a flail.
Consciousness emphasizes
a break-even aesthetic, i.e.
We all need to be getting more sleep
as masculinist homily.

Our feet crunched on the walks
as if we were treading grain.
Or as if we were walking on fragments
from an enormous shattered mirror.

We keep pulling shards of glass
from our feet. If we don't,
they will work their spectral ways
into other, more intimate places.

You said you liked the crypt
best, because none of the objects there
bore any identifying marks.

The grand jury rejected the artifacts
I presented. Do you have any
other artifacts, the foreman demanded.
No, I do not have any other artifacts,
I replied, under oath. Was I lying?

❧

Why does Time have to be a woman, you ask.

All these interiors of soap and marzipan.
It's not that almonds contain arsenic, rather
that arsenic smells like bitter almonds.
So the stories tell us, the ones
with the clowns and dinosaurs. We see bodies
as something frangible, interchangeable,
like roadways. *Toll,* the British term
for what we would otherwise call
a rotary, a roundabout, a traffic circle.

The moral imagination is not lacking
for pageantry: all those troops of secondary
angels, bearing flaming fiberglass swords.
They're trying either to get into or out of a country.

Ask yourself: is it your country? Do you
belong there? Does gender? Do gods
step into God, into the idea of God,
and we pray to them the way we pray to a muscle
contraction, a broken arm, a broken rib?

We identify a weakness in the body
and we address it, as if it were a person, as if
the body were a separate person. What happens
vs. what might happen, should have happened.
We take our bodies out for walks,
to the supermarket or the travel agency.

◈

One of my students writes and asks me
what's just outside the window of wherever
I happen to be reading his e-mail.
I look up. I'm at a small library in Scotland
and all the windows are heavily blinded,
like horses, I think, stupidly, and blink a little.
I make something up for my student,
something about an old woman
with a walker, oncoming bands of light rain.

(But why does it have to be a woman, you ask.)

On the radio, a novel is a sheer surface
from which bodies try very hard to depend.
They're failing, mostly, but everyone
pretends not to notice, because it's so pretty.

If "the room in which one lives
anticipates one's burial in a Christian plot," then
the novel also, conceived as a sort of room
in which one lives. For a little while.

Are there more planets or more new planets
(cf. Piaget)? Are there more races
or more profiled races? Are there more
bodies, more bodies, more bodies? Are there?

◈

I want to turn the noise upside down
and step inside it, the way one steps inside
a giant trash bin to tamp down
the garbage. Superimposition of body on body,
on the warm, aspiring body noise breaks.

If a body disappears inside noise,
does it simply become part of the noise—
now a larger noise, an augmented
racket—or does it simply cease to exist,
I mean as a body? Does it translate
into mere memory of a body
(i.e., dependent upon other bodies)?

Memory as a function of the body,
a little dance painting allows
inside the castle. The moral imagination
struggling to don its superhero costume,
form-fitting, skin-tight.

It's not like that, you say, and I want
to believe you, because we're here together,
in our glorious, refurbished kitchen.

We've lost the corpse, the angels cry, and
Whoops, there go the fiber arts.
Memory is an object, and the bodies wrap it up
in whatever lies closest to hand:
flesh, silk, parchment. Paper or plastic?

❖

How speech works: the body co-opts
language and vamps a matinee performance,
i.e. the body holds language up
in front of itself, as if it were a mask.

Sometimes language, like napalm,
melts into the face, throat, chest,
genitals of the speaker. Unlike napalm,
this can seem painless. Some people
don't notice until the performance
is over. Some people never notice.

Sometimes a mask keeps talking
long after the negotiating body
has retired, fallen away or disappeared.
(Call this literature.)

Sign language: merger of body
with mask. It's why some of us find
the deaf so threatening, so Other.
A gender we haven't sexualized yet,
a plane crash dooming an orchestra.

Here, listen to this, you say.
I take the headphones. It sounds
like a bunch of planets talking.
It *is* a bunch of planets talking, you say.
Sometimes the world impresses,
merely through superior fidelity.

❖

Habeas corpus, meaning, we're still here!
and having our share of authority issues
on the affective level. The Pre-Raphaelites
have been reduced to a costume drama
nobody is watching even though everybody
has an opinion about how campy it must be.

One body poses for a painting by another
and we can document this, e.g. deploy
photography or its more active cousin, film.
Language (Light. Faith. History).
waits outside the building. NO LOITERING
read the signs, but language doesn't care.

Language has no problem with its own
superhero costume, which we call
gender—the idea that somewhere,

somebody is feeling something
other than what you yourself are feeling.

Language has an idea of rest, but it can't
quite find the words to express this.
Which is funny, when you think about it.

At least some of us long to be defeated
by the body or its agents, the angels.

Is gender, then, a lyric form, ventriloquy
of the body and its clastic fashioning? Or is it
just another prop, left over
from some other landscape, some other film?

❖

Our story so far: we were planets, and
somebody made a movie. Either we were
or were not in it. People in it
had sex and wore clothing, some of which
viewers referred to as "costumes."
Language was implicated, alongside
a god or gods. Predicate: to have made
a movie, to have been in a movie,
to implicate, to have been implicated.

Our story so far: a sign or map
of where ghosts have been, their proteins.
A painting or a sculpture. Icarus.

It's not enough to believe in the body
so long as the body believes in pronouns,
which are a sort of angel the body wears
in lieu of some more tangible mask.

I don't want to get boring about this,
because today—on this particular day—
I am otherwise busy mourning
someone I did not know well, but who
was nevertheless kind to me, once.
She died, far away from where I am.

Grief is a little church we don't remember
joining. Say the angels of language
who do not, as I understand it, grieve.

❖

In the castle, one of the British poets
suggests maybe Yukio Mishima had a point.
The other disagrees, almost violently.

If you surround yourself with the dead
then you worship the dead. What does it mean,
to believe in the dead in the same way
one believes in cheddar, oak, chlorine, things
that appeal to the senses?

An edge appeals to the senses
because it can be apprehended. We say
a leading edge, a floreate edge. We say verge,
we say ogham, we say
we want to get out more, get more exercise,
spend more time with the kids.

An edge means change, means we
recognize something. Possibly we've been here
before. Really, though, it's hard to say.

❖

If writing, then, is "thought's patience"
then consider the Picts, the way their men
touched their women, the women
their men, cathedrals have
their own histories but genetics concludes
there is no common ancestor.

Writing as occult practice:
the living talking to the dead, or vice versa.
The tedious invulnerability of language
through six or seven dimensions.

We keep taking photographs of children.
It's not just about capitalism,
air pressure, nostalgia. Tracking shots,
birthday parties, YouTube.

The army is a set of relationships
many of us have been unable to locate
inside the biological family: trust.
It is almost like love but it is not love.

I want to call out to you, but the intention
is all mixed up with blood and iron,
northwesterly tea of oxygen and lurid
expectation. The consecutive narrative
keeps picking up, breaking off.
Like holes in a leather belt, you said,
when the trains ran. Biology, fear's staggerlee,
its amplitude and registry, swift secretary.

❖

I begin to anticipate, that is, I begin
not to listen anymore, not to rely on the senses
but rather on hunches, superstition,
what we know we *think* we know we know.

When we know it. He said,
Don't worry, you'll recognize the place
when you get there, when you see it.
I'd forgotten
you have your own Yukio Mishima story.

Sometimes we hide from the films
the dead are showing, because
we're no longer certain whose side
we're on, who's up late at night
inside the museum. It's safe to say
faith runs the museum, in the sense that
you have to believe in something
to want to go view the evidence
of "something" in the first place.
Its vapor trail, its enameled shell casings
scattered around the crime scene.

I'm no longer interested in the crime,
just the scene, the accoutrements,
the props and dust enmantling everything.
The body makes everything
a painting of gender, and it's our night-job
to supply the thought balloons.

It's not just about memory,
eye/bee/flower. Nor is it a story.

And yet it's so comforting to think
about it: as a film, a painting, a story.

❖

You can step away from the vehicle
and *put the gun down*. Narrative remains
part of this story, wears deep grooves.

The pageant is a conjuration,
a magic lantern show of the species.
It's OK if you want to get up
and walk out. —You can't walk out.

Archaeologists remain divided
on how much photography
can tell us about how other people
groomed their animals,
their public health administrations.

When I was in the hospital,
possibly dying not from cancer
but from septic complications
resulting from a successful operation
to remove cancer, I did not think
about West Nile virus. Not once.

The flaming sword sets fire
to the paper it pierces.
Blackdamp, slatefall. Tap-tap,
the miners beating out their mortal
semaphores. We will interview
the survivors: if not the miners
themselves, then their
loved ones and their neighbors.

Only the rectors were buried in
the chapel walls. Also, their wives.

❖

Bits of skin, stand-ins for touch
in the mind's eye, in the projector's
flaring beam. Conditions of trauma
induce language, not silence.
But only in survivors.

We dedicate the stories to gender
whether gender wants us to or not.

The angels in the sconces,
in the roof bosses, in the capitals
keep playing their instruments,
holding their books to their chests.
Their expressions are wide-eyed,
breathless, as if they've come
a long distance, forced by a wind.

We haunt them, is what I think.
We are the ghosts they see.
They are terrified by our
imperfections. Among other things.

Poet as eyeclark. A disease
working its way through
language's body, first the muscle
fibers, then the neurosystem.
A disability. Congenital.

I had hoped, by now, to be a father.
I had hoped, by now, to be a husband
and type from these two offices.

Can a ghost haunt a haunting,
I ask. Only on the head of a pin,
you reply, and turn the glowing page.

PART IIIA
CHROMOTHERAPY & UNION

Almost midnight. This is the season
of long light, of matrices and geometry: *X* into *Y.*
We approach the podium, Help Desk
of the disentangled, the disengaged. Other animals: abide
for the sight gag, lead kindly (light).
A wholeness, or: *You there.* Abstract. Zenith.

The grief of language is that there is, finally,
no Other. Only the body, transposition
in scale and meter, black patch on which language skids.

At the end of topological space
money stands waiting, hips cocked.
The tongue feels around inside for something
to inject, comes away empty(-handed).

As an allegory of exchange, God-
visitor to this labyrinth. It was all so logical
in the sense that gender follows
some necessary turning. Columbine, columbarium.
Neo-Manichaean faith healing: we recognize one another
in the soldiers' reports to the capital.

❖

Language moves in circles. Every so often,
moments of unexpected eccentricity
suggest something else is out there. A ghost
in the puppet room stirs silk
into coffee and we call it
chromosomes. Or gryphon, whatever,
some mythological trope.

Do you think language cares,
you said, and "follow your discomfort."
Language quotes from other
language, absence in the form of a question.
MANUSCRIPT LOST IN WELL,
GO BACK TWO SPACES.
A bit of fur trim to the collar
that suggested, even to her nine-year-old
niece, something was probably
rather more exciting than what painting
was telling her just then

about ashes, her Catholic neighbors
red-hot in the glow of the mill, silk forehead
redecorating desire's invisible music.

❖

Before sleep, honey-skin
crimson with blackcurrant, 90p
Machin in royal blue. Meticulous
this hatred for the immaculate
conception, orogeny, usurer's bead
pending in plain view.

Predicate: to assert, affirm,
preach, declare. To have poisoned,
to have carried or clothed.

One must read aloud in a dark
country. The masks have grown
deep into their faces, shreds
of leather clinging to the dialect
of *I can't, I won't*. Faith
braids them, weaves them
into palimpsests, plans for houses

capitalism builds for the poor
on some dank Georgia floodplain.

Dream of bone movement, lactation
of language, dental almanac—UN-
DELIVERABLE AS ADDRESSED, NO
FORWARDING ORDER ON FILE.

A shriek is a lyric form, yes
or no. Saul and his thousands, David
and his tens of thousands.

History proofreads, binds the rare
earth elements, admires the blond grain
(maple probably). —Compass me.

❖

One impulse is to redraw the map,
another to redraw the body.
The British poet says he saw a baby owl
perched on a turret, above the castle.
"It couldn't fly," he said—
"Not yet" and "It was clearly terrified."

Starred wire of the breath curled
around each rib, protective.
Infestation of the motherlife, accrual
of species-specific dance notation.
Earth, air, water, fire,
Fibonacci: the great Atlantic rift, *see*
Prescript vs. postscript (gender as),

biology's concerto in the food court
among the wax-splayed vegetation.
A map of the terminal reveals
no sit-down restaurants with wi-fi

connections in the immediate
vicinity of this foundation-exchange
symposium. Therefore: language
fails the body? or vice-versa?

I keep drawing the same five-pointed
star in the margins
where race continues gleaning,
milk-blaze we can just
make out in the eastern sky. Not enough
God, I misread. Not enough rescue.

❖

I see you your Cherokee princess
and raise you a Holocaust. You do the math.

Genealogically, we are all now
native speakers of both English and
mathematics, so if you can't
balance your checkbook, kindly withdraw
from this Nation of Islam training seminar.

Because that's what we're talking
about, isn't it? Race as just another
paradigm of belief, another
bodhisattva. So you'd like to believe
in race. OK. Capitalism says it's OK.
Grief and AIDS both say it's OK.
Certainly the history of Western
jurisprudence says it's OK, OK, OK.

God, or our lack of God, says
no, probably not OK. A jealous herme(neu)tic
this Y-chromosome, minuscule spy.

❖

Norse chess set carved from whalebone
and found on Hoy, early medieval. All the figures
look vaguely hung-over, or as if they had
toothaches. You have to wonder who
had that much free time, in medieval Orkney,
and under what circumstances. Schrödinger's
text, collapse of language's wave function
at the hands of (Light. Faith. Boredom. History).

My conducting instructor contended
the human mind can only keep three errors
in conscious thought at once.
REPLY URGENT. STOP. Music doesn't care.
It caresses our cell phones as if
they're on leave from some dreadful purpose
where electricity is alive again,
vibrating in the night like a bevatron.

It's all OK, isn't it, one of us was saying,
and the light flooding in, nunlike and Québécois,
I mean, if we wanted it that way, a sort of building
one could walk up to, and peer into,
but never *enter*, because it wasn't made for that,
the Picts were so easy to convert
to Christianity even though nobody understands
why one species died out just as the other
was coming into its own, I'm talking
about the Neanderthals here, what I really mean is

Look, we even let them keep their caves.

❖

Alphabet, dream of inheritance:
not just this one (Western, English, Times
New Roman) but all of them.
Sequoyah if you like, Joseph Smith's

occult Egyptian. The Voynich Manuscript.
Accounts in arrears in Deutschmarks
or a wedding invitation, knight
to queen's four: music doesn't care.

My friend showed me her new tattoo,
a snippet of Hopkins on the inside
of the wrist. "I think he'd be horrified,"
I blurted. My friend, coolly:
"No, I think he'd like it, actually."

In the supermarket, bisected epigraph
on the rinds of pork or beef, in violet.
I avert my eyes, but it's hard not to read
a text that's presented to you as a comestible
protein source: this is the logic
of advertising. (Among other things.)

❖

Diva of indifference, sing for me.
I have my popcorn, my sacred fringe.
I have my little rituals and traditions,
only some of which historically involve
flaying the skins of other animals.

Reeds dipped in tallow: see
Light (obsolete prototypes for).
We can take back these
library books and take back the night
at the same time. We can evacuate
the hospitals as if there were
a bomb scare by calling up and saying
"BOMB," because
there's never enough skin to go around.
To go to ground. To run aground.
Sweet lullabies in the swan boats, O.

What do your people think about
climate change, the Irish novelist asks,
just as I was about to say something
about Jung, who, I'm told (later),
was a vicious man and mistreated his wife.

Prague's prayer wheel, its celadon
shawl. Do we really want to be
rescued, and if so by whom? Hochma
in syndication, Ground Zero for
Who exactly am I talking to, anyway?
Light, says light. Faith, says faith.
Language, says history. —*Gotcha.*

❖

The tongue dips inside apocalypse
for just a moment, tries it on and suddenly
all matter exists only as scar.
I don't think the rant is a lyric form, I say
to nobody in particular
who, as it turns out, is on her way
into the nerve system to check her e-mail.

Next station stop, Auchinderry.
Demolished paper mill. Is it cruel
to be dead, pyrography
of time upon consciousness.
Time is waving, it wants to get our
attention, wants to ask us out
offer us a swell investment opportunity
hit us up for loose change.
Fathers/sons, mothers/daughters,
this occult compression
(of animal, vegetable, and mineral).
Little brainwave stigmata,
organ pipe inside which Ernst Chladni

slipped liquid or colored gas
so that he could examine the effects
of sound vibrations in a medium.

Globalization means we are all now
the targets of somebody
else's vengeance, possibly our own.
What goes around, comes around
as chemical residue or else
some virus. I said *Icarus,* not Isaac,
though thank you for bringing out
the parallel. Signs in the airport:
FALSE CLAIMS OF ASYLUM
WILL BE PROSECUTED.

Clerical cymatics: 213 carved boxes
that might or might not yield
a motet, plate/diaphragm/membrane's
retail pattern for lute tablature. Exactly
99 rabbit pelts to stitch the rug
in the castle solarium—yes, I counted.
(—Men do that.) (—As you say.)

❖

After the Union County 4th of July parade,
one of my students was troubled.
Why did it have to be so spectacular, she said.
(A military plane buzzed in giant circles
overhead.) Because it works,
I said. The Nazis were exceptionally
good at it. Direct appeal
to the retina, without benefit of language.

But it *hurt* me, she said: I felt
as if I were hurting inside,
while I watched. —You watched, I said.

If the angels are really ghosts,
I postulated, then how would they dance?
Aurora borealis, you said
and I liked that, a gesture with light
outside of language or history.

I've seen the aurora twice:
once, at the edge of the Blue Ridge,
I thought it was terrorism
or I was having a stroke, I was dying,
radiant fuchsia ripples—
like a shower curtain
I couldn't stop myself from thinking.
The second time, in Iowa,
walking from one dark farm
to another, on a cold November night.
It formed an enormous,
white-green loop, like a marquee.
You'd think Jesus would come soon,
one of the men with me said.

Women were also with us.
I don't remember what they said.
I do remember one pointing,
the keel of her black shawl,
soft fragment a harp might dream of.

Sometime later you admitted
you'd thought you were answering
some other, different question.

❖

The first abundance, your whole life
symmetrical, as an interruption in the organic
progression of X into Y, matter
into fungible currencies the heart inhales, and

stops. Face it, I am so tired of your
tremulous monopoly on volition
as violation. The things you see that aren't there
are inscribed on the surface of
a god, your whole life, you can reduce
it to biology and the state if you want, and if so
good luck, capitalism is rooting for you,
grief and AIDS are rooting for you,
the pathetic fallacy is rooting for you
from its Gorgon-cave, splendidly appointed.

The matrilineal power of self-
obsession, I misread. Not once, but
twice. Dream-Kadath of
time stoppage through vedic holiness.

Another misreading: God's *viscous*
omniscience. It coats us.
Minuscule as a panopticon (and about as
demure), we're dazzled by the sheer glitz
of proliferating selves (and
yes, "fluoridated" has a "u" in it).
While we're here, what men talk about
when they can't talk about
themselves, or sex: fantasy baseball,
Nietzsche vs. Apollo. Who would win?

❖

One word stands for another,
Proto-Sinaitic. The bathroom
mezzotint shows a cockatiel clutching
what appears to be an apple paring
in its left claw, in its right
a magnolia in full bloom. Add these
to your Aztec calendar.

In negative space we are not
dead, we are not safe, we are not
free. In negative space we are
not, no flint, no clinker, no
flight of stairs leading up
to the terrace. We see it and our eyes
slide past, some drab set from a play
memory's past restaging. Not even
a real play, in a real theater:

Cowboys and Indians, cabaret
fatale, Capone in Chicago.
We fire back and the gun renders us
biography, the tenant
sleeping inside the doomed hotel
and the rag soaked in gasoline,
just before the spy lights (upon) it.
At midnight, ghost-trains
in the theater, chuffing in the wings.

Your body gets to choose:
the theater, the train, or the wings.

❖

The story so far: what musical
orphans we make! *A victory for intelligence*
the operatives telegraph
back to the capital, to the in(di)visible state.
The ghosts applaud, fragile curators
of junkies and florists. An argument being a long scar
anyone can feel, appendectomy
of a nationalized rail system. Very pleasant,
this automated steering mechanism.

We become confused. Apparently
the word *legume* means the same thing

in English as in French,
in French as in conversational Egyptian Arabic,
but not in English and in Arabic.

Forgiveness: why don't you.
Because there is no adequate basis:
no text, no mandate of the body
or its constituent organs. Measure the gaff
against your lifeline, delusional matrix, relief map
in which money pretends to believe.

The miners quit looking up once the pits
were deep enough. They couldn't see
their bodies   hurtling through pigment
through all the surfaces of music.

❖

Fuse in the Tarot deck, hidden
economy in which violence answers violence
and we feel, if not exactly *good*
about it, then satisfied, sated. Blood-lust
in the orchard, must we review the polysemy
of "cherry," of "apple." —But I am weary
of turning that violence inward,
towards the postures of violence, pretense
as explanation, *Whatever*, existential
VingCards into rooms with dark beaches,
natal slosh of mesh against structure.

We used to think the sea could purify
anything, given time and distance. Now we know
(apropos of the theological) that we
can kill anything
once: a speech, a kitchen,
a Hanseatic bill of lading sold on eBay.

The dream of origin has a name,
an unpronounceable name. A clerk admits
you into the concrete world and you
succor her, you suffer him, alongside gender
in its glad rags and bangles. History
records this obsessive preoccupation
with offal and thanatography and concludes
this bomb *is* going to go off, only
not yet. There is still electricity. There is still
that davening in the blood, heroic
counterpoint: one in the flock,
one in the corn, and someone watching.

Predicate: to have stood, to have waited.
In the lobby, among the vending machines.
You are surely in a movie somewhere.
To whom does one pray in such moments.

PART IIIb
ORE RIFT

The revelation that the Anasazi
were cannibals affected not so much
the Southwestern tourist trade
as the nature of its camouflage, e.g.
advertising. We insist on the particular.
That is, *I* insist on the particular, I.

In the Sierras I often hiked up into
the high passes to the old silver mines.
What I enjoyed was standing outside
the dark wedges
of their entrances. Some were large,
sculpted, braced in timber or quarried stone.
Some were merely holes, and some,
oddly, were sealed off by wooden doors,
little wooden doors set into the sides
of enormous mountains. Cue *Peer Gynt.*

The first gods mean to kill you
and thereby rejoice in the misfortunes
variously apprenticed to them, e.g.
synecdoche, the nightly news:
(Outside. Neutral. Disaster. Return).

Israel, your breath in January
moonlight, maps in four colors, cuneiform.
Except: Then what. Then what.

❖

To assay: put to the proof, try, test.
As by fire, or blame. Hard to be exactly

sure of your role when the newspaper
keeps arriving by private car, hour by hour,
infinite regress of Carthaginian exposure.
The animals tolerate one another
and we like it, we frame the limited-edition
print and hang it in the labyrinth.
The players pause, study, move on.

The security camera holds its breath,
starts counting as if every little extinction
were an apocalypse gender
had been imagining, bored, locked
in its tower of insolence and hair.

It's not as if I'm *defending* war, I say,
and you shrug again, as if to say
Me neither, why? Rather that sixteen boys
trapped in the pine forests of their bodies
will light fires, find a language,
then or in facsimile,
annihilate any rare-earth dream montage,
any roadside chapel. Mercury, Nev.,
deathwatch suburb of the nuclear state
now just waiting out the aliens.

❖

Via fragment, again, synecdoche: the part
for the whole and the whole, clastic,
like the model of the body's organs
in a hospital waiting room. I cannot
apologize for the body's sugar
synthesis, its pale, dismantled stallion
of proteins and hormones. Its flesh-pasture.

Thought-organ, eternity-organ:
Apprehend. (It is easier in fairytales.)

Orogeny, the formation of mountains;
orography, the study of mountains
though from the root it seems to mean
"writing with mountains." Über-
stylus for some text we sand down,
coal seam by coal seam.

Convulse vs. revulse, study in late Latin.
Language follows: obvulse, evulse, invulse.
Who keeps the young of the species
radiant, the body bathed in blood (literally)
a public exercise, a graduation.
Come out come out, wherever you are.

❖

The proprietary mask,
not so much specie as sensation, i.e.
discovery: in possession of what
nobody else has, not yet. Thus:
driven by narrative, concealment
vs. disclosure, that tête-bêche.
We've been here before. It ends badly.

Congratulations, you tell me,
from over my shoulder: you've
only used "fire" 33 times
in your poem, 41 if you count
"fires," "fire-tongue," "firelight,"
"firetruck," "fired." (and now 47.)
Only once have you yourself
set fire to something, a story,
a null set, a nonce triangulation
you don't believe in anyway.

Language masks. (Light. Faith.
Ambition. History.) Ergo, duration:

dilation of time in earth tones,
plangent bass diaphony, organum.

❖

You chose not the owl, Raptor
    but the owlette, Raptor-in-Training.
The acquiring angel in his combat fatigues
    notes the tenderness of the exposed
pelt, small sores of subculture,
    catastrophe. What splendid animals!
exclaim the prisoners in the castle
    drawing-room (so rudely forc'd: no,
replete in their epaulets, their insignias).
    If you "feel powerless" then
may I present to you the five senses
    in which power works its embroidery
of gold thread across the sublime
    surface of your physical person
over which the law hovers. The riddle
    is not where in the body time
seeks to build its humming nest:
    the riddle is that out of all the animals
only we have developed a form
    of representational language. Us
and the bees, which are, of course, dying.

❖

To try by touch or by tasting. Archaic,
one who tastes food and drink
before it is passed on to his superior.
(Use of the male pronoun as per the original.)
The material world rubs against us
and we hold elections,
plastic in the aesthetic sense, a photocopy
of a photocopy in acetate and rust.

In the archaeology of race
the material world staggers zombie-like
among the oblivious townspeople
on their way into and out of the labyrinth.
They're not surprised one of the stars
is half-beast (having been prepared
by the constellations and hotels,
the bitter arcade flotsam of youth).
They race past the dark aviary
at the center of town without recalling
which key the wind had tuned to
when the school bus filled with children
plunged over the embankment
or into the firetruck, or through
the caution barriers at the rail crossing.

The ghosts sidle through the puppet
theater and touch the marionettes
lightly, run their ectoplasmic hands
over the strings as if hoping
for some audible effect.
We in the audience can't see them
but we know we're hearing something
we're not actually hearing.

Touch, taste; taste, touch. See the
high-quality orpiment, the vintage lapis
applied to the nerves of the neck
through audition, light
glancing off the hair's-breadth
heddle knotting foot to ankle, shin to knee.

It is not quite the opposite of dancing.

❖

The little ore carts—one on display
in downtown Bishop, California—
presumably required
somebody to push, or somebody to pull.
Primitive smelters in the valley,
arrastre the Spanish called them,
teeth in the otherwise unhinged jaw
of the high meadow country
we labor towards. Broken bottles.

In Roslin Glen, the ordnance map
plots "weir" where the gunpowder
factory sluice cut through.
Now it's a nice place for shamans
I mean Hamas I mean young mothers
with their prams and gossip. BOOM.

I don't understand the link
between imagination and intention,
the Boston editor writes to me,
and later: the *ineffectiveness*
of imagination vs. the *unimportance*
of intent. But I am in Scotland

and no, a tear in the retina is not
gendered, which is why my friend
Karen in Lagos has undergone surgery
and also my brother Myron in Pa.
is undergoing the same surgery
two weeks from now, assuming, that is,
his retina does not completely self-
destruct in what we call the meantime.

So if you want to be a predator
you emerge into this unworld
of taxation and caudal citizenship

which you can wield in your loneliness,
including the tall bodies of others.

❖

It would have been easy to mistake
this place for a source of silver
or gold, possibly even uranium
once the atomic age kicked in.
I mean, for one thing, there's this
castle, and for another, the owls,
raptors with their night-vision.
They have to be deriving substance
from somewhere, somehow.

From the castle tower, we watch
all the (other) animals watching us.
On rainy days this is diverting.

Predicate: nodal patterns
used in the design and construction
of acoustic instruments—
violins, guitars, cellos.
A little powder on a taut surface,
Eine Kleine Nachtmusik.

See, there in the dusty vitrines
of the municipal museum: pickaxe,
assayer's scale. Not a bad place
for the blind, assuming they still
have use of their natural hands.
Here, fossil fuels removed as ribs
from the chest of the planet—

They have somebody to taste
their meals for them, you observe, out
walking against the wind. *We* don't.

◈

High above us dense clouds
of particles discharge their energy
into the atmosphere, and we love them
for it, we will always love them.

There, finally: something to love.
But do they not love us back?
No, they do not love us back.

The pearl does not love you back,
the novel does not love you back.
Mathematics loves the subatomic
particles inside of you, that *are* you, but
individually and would tear you apart
like Tinkertoys (remember the original
racist packaging?), like Lincoln Logs
(absurd historical reference)
in order to love them more effectively.

Gold loves us—silver too—but only
in quantities, and in very bright light.

You could trip, hiking in the desert
at night, and fall right into
one of those old prospects, you noted.
Meaning: the earth loves us
back, loves us back, loves us back.

◈

If I said I loved you back, I would,
of course, be lying. If I said I.

First there was only a name
attached to the video, and then a second

name—misspelled, it turned out.
Eventually a full name,
an address, a biography.
—But it looked so fake, a friend said.

I watched the video
over and over, I read the articles.

She took singing lessons. In another
part of the desert, in the capital.

❖

To smelt: the eye: croft of images
annealed, as if by lading, the dream's factual
disembarkment. Invisible body
of the perpetrator seared, in some myths
a god who drank blood in the night, in some
a trickster. Yes to the future, its outrage
of brushed aluminum and glass. We dreamed
of falcons, kestrels, eagles soaring
amid these man-made canyons. Not for long,
as it turns out. (It always turns out.)

Your poem is not a target
so you write a longer poem and declare
"Now they must make of my poem a target."

A delicate silver instrument draped
in a black shawl is one way of phrasing it.
Three deer swift against a garden close
and men running, they're not sure
why, they have no guns, nothing
but deer, the idea of deer. Something to see.

Atmosphere encrypts twenty-seven
sodium vapor lamps

while we watch! Place your bets:
The Cherokee did not practice the ghost dance.
Animal to police, painting to predicate
(to have written, wanted, read).

Palpate her throat. You know you want to.

The trial begins. You go as spectator,
get called
to the jury box, to the witness box,
to the defendant's seat, to the judge's chamber.
Outside the courthouse, the hills are
alive with orange flame. *In this rifted rock
I'm resting,* beautiful country burn again.

❖

We are asked to choose between the men
and the men. Yes, this is a problem:
the moral imagination on dialysis,
bent low over its block of obdurate stone.

This problem of gender, a chisel.
You will take a new name from a man
if you privilege the antiquity of his song
(for medicinal purposes).

And if the blood (for medicinal purposes).
And if the silence (for medicinal d°).
And if the rain (for medicinal—you get
the idea, it's not a large one, emotion
beats against the walls of the pineal gland
but MapQuest gets us there on time).

❖

We move inside the inanimate and
devise rules, those magnificent Rossettis,
the approved script specifies
a quaint ethnic tonsure
down which soldiers climb, *Rapunzel*
a glyph you don't speak, breathe rather
as the tongue makes its slow way
along the glabrous inside of a glove.
(Language watches attentively
from its manacle chair in the labyrinth,
in full surround-sound stereo.)

Trade: to make a wish, to examine
for the sake of information, to learn
or know by experience, to try
with affections, temptations, force.
To assail with words, arguments, love-
proposals. A glyph for this: "money"
crossed with "world," *Weltgeld.*

You get to choose: The light.
You get to choose: The language.
History, not so much. Faith?

In Nevada, it's illegal to reveal
the locations of ancient petroglyphs.
In California, it's legal, but nobody will—
just a vague wave into desert wash
towards bridal chamber, birthing cave.

And so they went up again
to Nablus, to Bethesda, to Jerusalem.

—Here, try this, you say. It's good.

❖

Choice in a bar, on a quay,
in the basement of the old rectory,
among the musty hymnals. (Some music
lives in the tongue,
some has its mail forwarded.)

A CHILD IS NOT A CHOICE
the decals on the 18-wheelers read
and this seems indisputable, I mean
as an assertion taking place
in language, grammatically correct.

If you are reading this and feel dead
then you have a choice, a wing
on which gender prays
something like nine times a day.
This oriency, this brilliance, this luster.

Artesian well in winter.
The cattle are lowing, the baby awakes
just in time for his passport photo.
Even her nine-year-old niece knew
she was too poor to afford that coat.
Somebody gave it to her, her mother
explained, and that was all.

❖

We live in bodies, unlike, say, Sagittarius,
agitprop of the machine spectrum
funicular glands and a shake of the dice
cup's museum-quality astragals.

Edvard Munch drew light-lines
nobody else could see and called them
disembodied bell-curve spectra.
—No he didn't, not in English anyway,

but you feel it, don't you?
The mood lighting, the zodiac rung?

Pretty orphans, decked out for Christmas.
The law of magic says imagine
cherubim, now imagine them as friendly fire
you can't scrape from your clothing,
phosphorescent cutouts in the cardboard
of old refrigerator boxes.

In Cassiopeia's house, scorpions
cover the floor, some living, some dead.
Nobody seems to notice.

Here, the latest of her sheet music scrapbooks.
She's a conscientious collector.
All that time in the night sky, choice
is something she's heard of. She's interested,
you have her attention. Go on, tell her.

❖

You can't hear what the dead are saying
because they are still trying to speak
in the language of predators and men pressed
from bread, from a broken academy.

Here are some rules for any extra ribs
you may find lying around: use as clavicle,
bowsprit, as assisted walking mechanism.
As corset stay. As architrave.
As musical instrument. As target for lasers
you train. As subject for future artwork
or dramedy. Really they are very useful, ribs.

The dismemberment of the saints
is a historical fact

only if you believe in all their relics.

The puppets jerk in their even-drowse,
their shellacked boxes of camel-hair velvet.
They know something photographs don't
about the refugee camps, the blueprints
for the high school gymnasium destroyed
by fire. Letters addressed to the body
are returned to the body, COD.
The tribal version is also available,
shreds of bone and clothing asperged artfully
in the bio-muck by the Japanese concessionaire.

Known as "the father of acoustics," Chladni
was also the first modern scientist
to seriously propose that meteorites
originate in space, rather than terrestrially
in the gullets of active volcanoes.

❖

Some powder, then, on a membrane;
some basic sand. The dream hums along
in its register of grit and peppermint and we see
more Green Men! is one explanation,
masculine counterpoint to the sheila.

We want to imagine something older
than Christ because (a) we've made Him
very small, (b) we don't want
to be saved (see CHOICE), (c) we want
to believe the original was inhuman
or, alternately, too human, not human enough
or not in our sophisticated human way.
The dream of the primitive:
once we all lived in the forest
where nobody died, the animals spoke

in languages we understood, and everybody
got plenty to eat. Wasn't it nice?

And it's true, or close enough, only
we weren't there. An idea of us,
rhizome in the reedbeds and the redbuds.
And a flaming sword this idea of us
mistook for a sun, in the night watches.

Susanne Langer: "A symbol
which interests us *also*
as an object is distracting." Carla
Harryman: "Did we live in a constellation?
Did it explode?" —Every particle
of music swept up, as if by ants, and hoarded.
We pick through lentils and ashes
(or better yet, have the help do it).

I am not saying the body doubles.
I am saying we were children once
and wanted something like fire, that wasn't
fire. Rachel Zucker: "I'm sorry, but there is
no new place for anyone to touch me."

❖

Night. Nablus. Nebulous. Jacob's Well,
a Cistercian brotherhood
for coercion. Inside your thumb
is another thumb: here, the sidewalk art
proves my point in garish 3-D.
No longer can I "jew" you down on
anything, and "gyp" is in taste almost
as bad—but I can still call you "thuggish."
The power of Caucasia is also
a function of distance, of time and space.

So you choose fate, I mean faith.
(*Und der anderen Maria.*) The sphinx
asks her riddle, and you ride off
into the sunset,
stage-struck, precocious in your role.

Some Christians believe the dead
will rise with their constituent atomic
particles intact. This creates yet another
set of problems, imbrication
of matter, and matter's children.

Yes, I watched many different versions
of the video. Hoping
there would be some different
outcome? Yes, I suppose. Or
some different context. Some explanation.

We pare the maps away from the body
with only the sharpest of knives.
"Context" is not the same as "explanation."
Inside your second thumb is a mirror.

◈

Fresh from chromotherapy
we wash the black and white residue
from the backs of our hands.

You ask me, Did my relationship
with my sister "improve"
after she came to see me
on what she thought was my deathbed.
It's more accurate to say
that after that, we *had* a relationship.
She asked me to dinner once in
Las Vegas, a four-hour drive each way

across a desert, a bruise in the archive,
more undeveloped film. I went.

Magritte's art consisted of
identifying archetypes, isolating them
and then repeating them, in various
combinations, over and over again.
We "like" his paintings
not because they're good paintings
but because we recognize something
it feels as though we'd forgotten.

Cylindrical, conic, azimuthal.
"The familiar Mercator projection
has many advantages
in spite of the great distortions it causes
at the higher latitudes."
Clarke's spheroid of 1866.
Chronic landscape fatigue, the republic.

A face burns a hole in the retina
and we call it *memory,* or
obsession. Peel back the eyegrain.
Gentle solfège of the pulse,
close your soul. Now open it again.

❖

It's hard not to take one's gaze
off the ambient's threadbare perimeter.
The ribs, fingers resting
lightly on the lungs' abacus. How long
did that take to paint, in dabs and daubs?

The deer people are silly, yes,
and not very bright
but we follow them when no better

option presents itself. A wrong turn
on the ice: bruised spleen,
something calculated, a tally
of dirigible hydraulics,
sum and carry. The deer people
nurse their young like we do.
When I wear my dead president mask
they're no more afraid
than we know they already were.

Faintish data receptors, the tongue's
awash in what now? Only
a little bleeding. Or do you want me
to bring you something already dead,
G. Hill: "And—yes—Lilith
we have met | and do I know you?"

❖

A brief word about Marx (Karl).
He was a child once and
London was a story Dickens was telling
Boston, in all the best magazines.
The gods contain both male and
female, and survive thereby in time.

Prescription vs. description:
elementary. If you don't care
the rhetorical cleavage
evaporates, why *not* exile
in some brutal Irish laundromat
patrolled by sadistic nuns.
Yes, it was (is) horrible.
No, we should not blame our bodies
lightly. Circumambient:
appetite for formula, something
that will lie flat and be easily read.

Parchment, vellum, anorak.
Something to wear in the rain.

❖

It was a *Mormon* desert,
the man at the pizzeria explained to me
(by way of adding context, I guess).
Bishop, California segregated
in three wedges, tourist/Mormon/Paiute.
Our clothes grow on us
like transparent lichens, a symbiosis
of affect and colonial inheritance.

At least Joseph Smith understood
the need for a new alphabet
to make his point, also a semi-private
translation mechanism.
The best archives expand outward
from a single frame of film
projected onto the rear wall of a cave
and allowed to stutter there.
Entire governments follow this plan.

You remember love as something
like fire, but not fire, exactly.
More like a transponder, you say.
Little black boxes, glass negatives
on which the skeleton imprints cleanly.
The Nephites: said to be South American
Jews granted eternal life, or else
vague dust-devils in the desert

but we move so slowly
in this vicious, unfriendly climate
it's hard to map that motion.
We make easy targets
from the mesas, the mined-out cliffs.

Hey you, yes you there on the hillside,
you in the defiled pharmacy
of inheld breaths and adrenal hush money:
drop the tablets. Drop them now,
while we preserve this one
primitive emotion. It's all we have.
That, and absurdly complicated
water rights. Some cattle we can't trust.

❖

Presumably there is love there:
Mormon love, tourist love. Paiute love.
Survival is a thing Mormons learned
early, and how not to split
the body from the intellect. (Organon:
an instrument of thought
or knowledge, of the soul or mind.)

Not a *tame* Cartesian space,
the beaver said.
(Faith. Language. Light. Mystery.)

More about the Nephites, courtesy the *American Folk-Motif Index*:
"Nephite is described as a venerable man with saintly mien and very
clear complexion." "Nephite is an old man with a white beard."
"Nephite wears ordinary clothing." "Nephite wears white." "Nephite
invisible to some bystanders." "Nephites provide food miraculously
for those in need." "Nephites heal or prevent illness." "Nephites
bring spiritual message or uplift or prophecy." "Nephites travel with
miraculous speed." "Nephites disappear miraculously." "Nephite
appears in several places at once." "Food which Nephite has eaten
is discovered to be untouched after he has gone." "Nephite leaves
no tracks in snow."

—Pretty nifty, those Nephites.

The Egyptian novelist disputes
the place of the image in contemporary
Arabic poetry, i.e. Adonis, Mahmoud
Darwish. A particularity of vision
reduces the violence, but only
in terms of perception, that is, scale.

❖

Sky Burial, my friend is thinking
of entitling her new manuscript,
now that the Palestinians
have the right to choose. I'm less
sanguine, more phlegmatic.
Glasgow of the 1930s is in my veins.
We take from the desert, and
the desert waits. That's why saints
went there. You're wrong
not to touch them, the tour guide
told us, gently but firmly.
Of course they are there for you.

(A poetry that honors the distance
it transposes. Or subverts it. This,
then, the moral imagination.)

St. Swithin's Day, the British poets
come together now to dine,
the expat poet, the Irish novelist
and the Egyptian—we're all standing
together in the photograph,
lightning flashing in the background.

We have to get out of here,
music is humming, if only to itself.

It hurts, the doctor explained
from his shabby clinic in the desert
—in answer to my question
(and with a strange look on his face,
almost pity but not quite)—
because once there was something
there, and now there's not.

PART IIIc
THIS MITIGATING HAPPENSTANCE

In the scaffold of the wound
love's heart lies, many-throated messenger.
We are all hopeless idiolects, winter vowels
mute in the biceps. *Carpe diem,*
more petty inscriptions on the abdominal wall
drumming in its constituent dusts.

Where there was experience, let there be
experience. Race lengthens the distance
between the body and its
other, sleeping body while tightening
sleep's scuttled cords.

Carpe diem, "human eyes
or humanlike." Houses clamber into
new birthing technologies
and lie there, panting, in the clock-dark:
Keep your head down, sister.
A sign in the old city center reads

Tell me the name of this new resurrection.

❖

The doll, shaken (then forgotten),
leans into its floor-length
hunter-gatherer epoch, its plastic eyes
something that crawled out of a bowl of cherries
or some brochure about vacations of the future.
It is tired of sleepwalking and the men
and women who wear Michael Jackson
pinned to their lapels.

The archaeologists lurch and stammer:
this was never their free-trade enterprise zone.

To the doll, all things are doll:
horses, jewelry, our misplaced affections,
unmatched bonus socks from the laundry.

No one ever thought of setting a sci-fi apocalypse
in a Siberian nursing home
before Antoine Volodine did, and made it
an opera about Marxism, the end of time
and yes, misplaced affection. —Of course, nobody
bought his book (in English, anyway).

Away with you, Brigham Young, American.
There is war again in the world and you
are entirely too Emersonian
for this wound, this ghost flower, this iron chest.
You see and believe. Blessed is he
who does not see and yet, somehow, believes.

❖

My Joseph Smith doll, my Brigham Young doll.
Ann Lee is still trying to save us
from gender, dear misguided soul that she is.
She incorporated dance into worship
(or someone did in her name)
and straight-backed chairs as spiritual discipline:
YOU BREAK IT, YOU BUY IT.

—All right, my Ann Lee doll too
brooding softly over grammar's enemy aircraft
installation. Do you have a photograph,
you ask.   —Yes, but not of her, I reply.

If someone wants a photograph
give them a photograph, is the easiest way
to make faith work. Put your hands on your head,
put your hands in your head,
place your hand inside the puppet head
into his wounds. His wounds. Mr. Bojangles.

❖

New studies suggest my conducting teacher
was wrong: memory holds seven
(+/- three) things at a time.
This should make for more and better music
among other, more necessary things.

What's more necessary than music, you ask.
(Faith. Hope. Charity. ~~History.~~)
Predicate: four graces in three acts,
with accompanying Dadaist defenestration.
Boneless calves glimmer
in earth's rotational rent-a-tomb.

It is not like belief. Nothing is "like" belief.

Scientists hold glass slides
of the animals' skin tissue, hair, bone samples
up to the light and see
light, interruptions
in light. We are judged by the quality
of the interruptions we make in the light.

A poetry of reflective silence, cyanotypes
of mussel shell and doily, the body
pressed directly into the reactive medium.
We spot them on hillsides, amateur mycologists,
ornithologists, lepidopterists
now looking down, now looking up.

Scar as ghost-wound, proud flesh
burning in the twin nostrils of the cooling towers.
Naphtha, borax, creosote,
all you inferior forms of radiance, listen:
hum vs. pulse, alternating current vs. direct
participation in the glandular Colosseum.
Place your bets ladies, gentlemen,
vicars, purveyors of nutritional supplements:

in the gym of the bone,
in the gym of the rib of the bone.

❖

Incompletion, then. Insoluble
because any formal arrangement of elements
can be viewed as "complete"
on its own terms. Form brokers form.

Archaeologists suggest a second oval of standing
stones once stood outside the extant ring
and possibly there was a cairn in the middle.
Possibly something was stored in the middle
and possibly this something was a body.

To build vs. to erase, as protocol, ritual.
(Mandatory Rauschenberg reference:
SELF-PORTRAIT WITH ERASED CAIRN.)
Not even accounting for the cupmarks,
inscrutable little flagella of intent.

Intention perceives limit, imagination
none. To harry the intelligence,
sole intent. Form brokers form, and we fight over
the results, and from this a politics emerges,
leisure options, chestnut geldings on the beach.
And then what. And then what.

❖

Petroglyph of a circus train,
that which convokes wonder, including loss.
We commemorate. My own (lone)
memory of the Mojave
green, in full bloom, of generative possibility.

Sir William Sinclair, who built Rosslyn Chapel,
had hounds named Help and Hold.
Each noun, each *very*, each imperative a myth,
something to hold onto, believe in.

Where do you live, the ghosts keep asking.
In the forest. In the castle. In the chapel.
No, in the desert (of the real, thank you
Jean Baudrillard, also Slavoj Žižek
for your guided tour
of celluloid, a film in which a white man
talks about other films. Infinite regression).

But where do you *live*, a tourist
(another tourist) demands of me in the chapel,
on the steel catwalk encumbering the chapel,
the sort of glove a tongue fits into.

I live in a film of the desert. Help and Hold,
my faithful ghost-companions.

I drove through the desert for hours
and came out at Needles, because Alice Notley
had been from there, was born there.
It existed, therefore Alice Notley existed.

Eye/bee/flower. That moire. Even here.

❖

An unblemished skin: complete.
Or, incomplete. A wound in skin: complete,
an action, itself. An aesthetic mark,
a medical urgency. Eventually,
a scar: complete. There is no "incomplete."

In one version, the only eternal thing
made by man is a wound.
(You don't need me to tell you this.)

Photo-graphein, to write with light's
brief history, etch into plate
with matter's crude stylus, to reveal love
in the moment of loving, its emblems, its vessels.
The innovation of the Polaroid camera
was to bring the event
and the recorded evidence of the event
into almost-simultaneity.
As if there really were such a thing
as *love*, and we were just there, weren't we?

❖

In the passenger seats over the wing
we felt the swaying
as we accepted our meals.

Black box at the bottom
of continental drift, pinging out
its bell-like semaphore.

The aurora in the kitchen,
I thought I heard you say. No,
you said, nothing like that

and it is not about race, and
maybe it is a little bit about gender,
completion's incompletion

and maybe we invite it into the castle
where it flickers in the firelight.
A book enters a mountain

and doesn't come out, is one problem.
Friendship is another, severed hand
in a painter's portfolio:

It's a dream of a painting
I can't paint, she says, when asked.
The body exhales, relieves itself.

What is that, then, in the kitchen—
Another species trying to clothe itself
in some model of the universe?

Built to scale the legend read
when we walked on board the ship,
milk-slat, milk-lath, milk-lathe. . . .

To try by tasting, to touch
without touching, *Mitwelt* vs. *Weltgeld*
I told the animals, in the dream.

God visits a painting of policemen
and graphs sleep vs. advertising
(History. Language. Contact. Faith).

It is only a *novel* while you
are reading it, you tell me, gently
placing a hand at the back of my neck.

We give the colicky child a photo
to suck on, to comfort him.
It seems to work, most of the time.

—But where shall we wander,
my parents ask, hugging themselves
against the stiff desert night.

The final element in a series
accrues the value of all preceding
elements in that series,

the stewardess patiently explains.
What will we do when we get there,
inside the painting where God is?

Predicate: to have not yet
entered that picture, to have avoided
detection. To have excavated

the animals from their differences.
I can't see the end of this
Venetian interior, you murmured.

We hear the animals breathing.
The signs read NO PHOTOGRAPHY
ALLOWED IN THE CHAPEL.

❖

Outside the ghost, completion steps forward
into the clearing in the forest (Castle.
Chapel. Suburb). It is wearing its gender mask,
triple negation of this Western enterprise.
In some languages gender is intrinsic
to the mode of address, to grammar: words decline
in the masculine, the feminine, the neuter.

English is holding out, English reserves judgment.

Pathology of differentiated grays,
the map reproduced in every economy of solitary
persistence. *The minister will now take*
questions, says one animal to the other animals.
One: why this spirit exchange hoovering
all this existential lint from the carpet? Another:
what about the casinos, I know they suck
substance from the polity but I do like
the exquisite, inexpensive dinners they serve.
A third: when I woke up this morning,
I found blood in my urine. Will I die?

Yes, says completion, from outside the ghost.
Yes. and: Yes. Cadence, though:
music's own stab at grammar, at detection
vs. ancient cultures bent on abreaction
within the parameters of fair market value.

Is cadence a scar or is cadence a wound.
Please tell me why I feel this pain inside my wrist.

You can blame it on technology if you like.
You can change names to protect the innocent
if this makes you feel slightly
taller, slightly better, slightly more in touch
with your vestal remnant, your binding-spell.
(In the beginning was the Word.)

Can gender be a lyric form? Completion: Yes.

❖

Autochthonous with the state, biology's
concertina wire. The musicians
shift uneasily in their stiff Velcro straps,

reach for their platinum instruments.
They are not thinking about the dead
or if they are, only as a sectarian
progression of mathematics, i.e. form.

From the loudspeakers, ragged sounds
of birds. Either somebody is broadcasting
birds, or they are nesting in the boxes.

Everything starts to spin into the grain
plucked ripe from the field. Tool/utensil/
instrument: I *would* do this, do that, I *would*
accomplish. This business of fear
which hides inside biology, germinant.

If I say, I do not believe in the living
dead. If I say, the dead are an imaginary
stretcher upon which the living are carried.

Long lines of the living waiting
to vote, in Knoxville, Wandsworth,
Soweto. Language is thirsty, you say.
I don't know what this means.

Biology holds one end of the stretcher.
Who holds the other?

I ask completion: what does this mean,
that language is thirsty? Completion: Yes.

❖

Transverse Mercator, so that we
can see the cities better. We had almost
forgotten about the musicians, anxious
in their bonds. Some of them are male
and some of them are female. Presumably

they call out: to each other, to absent
loved ones, to their instruments.
To their captors, also presumably, though
in languages we don't understand.

They are neither blind nor blinded,
but they do not appear to see
biology, which moves among them, spooning
soup or blood into their open mouths.
The clearing is getting crowded
with all these animals, wold of undergreen
through which midnight sluices.

Some of the musicians are very young,
eight or nine. Their voices among the others,
calling out for their parents, perhaps.
To be so young, and yet—to understand
music. Time comes behind biology
and sprinkles a faint, almost imperceptible
dust on the bodies of the musicians.
When they cry out, the dust settles
in new patterns, which the animals study.

On the throat, and chest, and forehead,
wherever one tribe gathers. Is not
an altar, though one could call them that,
the places where the dust collects.

Would a new alphabet kill you, you ask.
A new painting, a new mask. A new memory
that grows outside of memory
like some sort of contagious paraclete,
a different or more sensual performance.

❖

The animals are leaving the clearing.
Every key to the castle opens one particular door,
but some open more than one.
Not everyone can get into the library.

Fulminant memorial to memory
beyond memory, history is light interposed
between biology and time.
At certain angles it resembles a sword.

You do not have to believe in the angel
in order to believe in the sword,
history whispers. It doesn't even have to be
a metaphor. It could be a real sword.

Only *if* it is a real sword, you have to
imagine it in motion, i.e. flashing
back and forth, as if someone were wielding it.

Who you imagine wields the real sword
determines the frequency at which
your cries are recorded,
the shapes they convoke (all over your body).
We have gone to war again. So
many patterns, so many shapes in the dust.

❖

The mirror inside my thumb itches.
It has worked its way up, from the heel.
It is trying to close over itself,
to form a scar. It is tired of reflecting
bloodwall, sinew and bone.

Outside their club, the unemployed miners
play rugby. Many of them are bald or balding.

A vast flickering above and behind them:
heat lightning. Or, the aurora.

One team scores, the audience cheers.
I keep missing the plays because
I am paying more attention to the distortions
at the edge of this picture, this screen.

I don't know you personally, I say,
and truthfully—but you mistake
my voice for a theater, and walk into it.

Inside the theater of my voice, you're
getting comfortable, munching popcorn
maybe. The lights go up.
(Soldiers stationed near the original
atomic test site could see the bones of their
fingers through their closed eyelids.)

Literature is one skin on which
dust from the wars keeps settling.
Gender is another. We make masks
from the materials at hand.

I wish I could see the movie. Maybe
in this movie love falls in love with love.

❖

When my friend died, he was on a bicycle
searching for a man he wanted to take care of,
whom he had been taking care of,
whom he felt responsible to take care of.
His heart failed him, literally.

His family buried him with his glasses on
and two or three ballpoint pens

in his shirt pocket, the way he used to wear them,
but otherwise in the traditional way,
i.e. we all helped cover the casket with earth.

When he appears to me in dreams
I listen very attentively to what he is telling me
although I know I won't remember, later.

I want your words, and your voice
in the act of making those word-sounds.
I thread my flesh between the plates
of the projector. It begins to burn. A map appears
on the wall, carmine calyx, Penny Black,
ruby-throated hummingbird.

A new nation creeps into the gaps left
by existing nations. An imbricating intelligence.

We have all been cruel, language is singing, and
You cannot hide from me.

Let us call this love, for a little while, after all.
That's it, hanging from the trees like hair.

❖

This exercise in micrographia, i.e.
you could be working to end world hunger
RIGHT NOW rather than reading
or writing poetry. You could be marrying
or being given in marriage. (Predicate: to give,
to have been given in marriage.)
You could take pleasure in the highway,
in the pleasures gender confers.

The dead cannot speak. Ghosts can speak,
but ghosts are not the dead.

The dead can touch, as ghosts cannot.
History: child-touch of language
inside of which the dead keep crying out
for their vanished instruments.

The libraries multiply, proliferate.
Locked out of one library, we find another.
Wedding rings on soldiers' hands
attracting subatomic particles, radioactive.

❖

Shall we render up the instruments,
the tools, the utensils, the fossilized tangents
of intention? Ghost-lips, the fire
having telegraphed its message
to headquarters, hunches into its haunches,
its electric calefaction.
Fire as a translation machine
whoever you are, wherever you live.

This instrument in brass, with a hook at one end
and a bell tethered to the other.
This one, all glass except for one silver bit
that might be a tiny, decorative fuse.
Maybe you're supposed to blow on it,
or into it. This one, of wood, almost identical
to this one, of clay. They occur in pairs.
We try beating them together.

Fathers and daughters, mothers and sons.
They're men, she said, I couldn't
even *take* them to a cosmetics counter.

Anything I say about God will be false
because I say it. Anything I say about God

that God already said about God
you will not believe, because I say it.

But remember: FALSE CLAIMS
OF ASYLUM WILL BE PROSECUTED.
I do not care for your humanlike
forms, mathematics is saying.
I have spoken too much about myth elsewhere.

◈

The gun fires, the box is opened,
the wave function collapses. We record all this
in language, of course
(with the occasional photograph).

Music, being a wave function, collapses.
Ghosts, being wave functions, collapse.

Hunger, being an appetite of the physical body,
abides. You cannot kill it with light.

Light seeps inside hunger and illuminates
(though in our haste and greed
we mistake its presence
for [History. Habit. Faith. Language]).

The gun, being a figurative construct
and therefore also a wave function, collapses.
I stood in the road at dusk
and let moths alight on my chest and arms.

In the wing socket of capitalism a little honey
is waiting to be made love to, slowly.

◈

The Egyptian novelist turns in his sleep.
He is almost lonely. He is dreaming
that he stands inside some large terminal,
waiting. He does not want to blame
anybody, not now. He does not whistle.

The British poets dream someone
is throwing a joint party
in their honor, only they're somewhere else,
at a pub, maybe, drinking alone.
It's one of their birthdays—
the other one's, each keeps thinking.

The Irish novelist lies awake and thinks
about her day job, as a reporter
for Parliament. Something about her work
strikes her as transparent, diaphanous even.
She is trying to understand
what physics is saying to her,
its whickering thaumatrope still inside
its cardboard box, price tag affixed.

And you. I have not even begun
to speak about you. There is a little more
room inside the garage where
we store all the disused works, the mines
and hospitals and amusement parks.

War comes close to calling us
by our real names. That's why we're
afraid of it, and yet attracted.

In the apartment where your cat died.
In the apartment where you won that award.
In the apartment where we both
made fun of the Jehovah's Witnesses, 2x2.

Four times, five times, the Pakistani sprinter
passes me on the village path.
It feels so unfair not to give him a name.

PART IV
INFOLDS & UNSPIRES

The footing of the human body is so complicated.
A kestrel breaks upward into beauty. Can gender be a lyric form?
If the river says so. The river says.

Is not God, is not one of the many little gods, innumerable.
Is not the body, but inheres within the body.

This question of appetite, of dietary laws.
A bit of broiled fish, to prove that one is not a ghost
infects the superanimate, the origin (as it were) of species.

Painters differ on whether the body of Icarus was recovered
wearing clothing, or what clothing it was wearing.
Identifying marks (wing shear).
Contents of stomach. Toxicology report.
Washed up as far away as Tasmania, New Zealand.
The girl remembers her mother said she was cold,
and then they were in the water a long time, sometimes together.

Enucleated, the body steals from the other animals
because an image tells it to? Allele for lactose digestion
moving slowly across western Europe
in time for colonialism, the triangular trade, *mfecane.*
Why does my wrist itch, why this particular
fire in the belly of language where gender rested?

Tender: easily affected, sensitive. By external physical forces
or impressions; acutely sensitive to pain, easily hurt.
Susceptible to moral or spiritual
influence, impressionable, sympathetic. Of a ship:
leaning over too heavily under sail-pressure,
"crank" rather than "stiff." Sensitive to pious emotions
or injury; touchy, nervous, ready to take offense.

The pageant revolves, but slowly, in time with an invisible music.

❖

The choreographers were the happiest
couple in the château. They were gay, so they weren't
attracted to one another, they said. Every day
they locked themselves into the factory of their art,
without benefit of music.
Because it's not about music, they said. It's about the body
and what the body can be made to do.

The factories of their bodies, moving into and out
of the scars intention draws
as if from some substratum of flesh. Art surfaces,
language surfaces (and we call it
Faith. Light. Arrogance. Ministry).

Tendable: ready to give attention, attentive.
Or, able to be tended, receptive; handy, able to attend.
Tenderling: a delicate person or creature,
a person of tender years, i.e. a young child. The soft tips
of a deer's horns emerging.

❖

Innumerable gods of the body, in the body
and we call them organs, meaning, organic to the body,
meaning, producer of sound when air is forced through.
(Chladni noted the patterns in the night sky.)
Periodically one of the gods gets sick, dies maybe.

An eagle lives in the glen, you said, and one of the British
poets quipped, that sounds like a folksong.

Biohistory, or: what happened to the original men?
Did they die; were they killed haphazardly, or in some more

systematic way. Did they move north, west
were they somehow simply (?) prevented from reproducing.

Two roots, Latin *tendere,* to stretch. Latin *tener,* delicate.
Well what more can you expect if it has two roots,
you say, looking up from your magazine.

The body sells itself, sells parts of itself
to science, to medicine, to duration, that is, an idea
of health. Watch how the animals crowd closely together
so that they can all appear in the photograph.

Pump his stomach, send the contents to the toxicologists.
Eat as if every meal should be your last.

❖

Root vs. rhizome, ramifying as from sources.
Moire, as overprint. (Those stamps no longer valid for postage.)
Or: seiche, intersection of wave motion in a medium
often caused on the surface of water
by earthquakes or other geothermal disturbances.

Other identifying marks: scars (multiple). Moles.
A bit of language, tattooed (on the inside of the wrist?).
Index finger on either hand slightly twisted
towards the far edge of the body, as if straining
to escape. Or averting its gaze.

Folksong as a map to race, as a race against maps.
Mammy's in the kitchen, fourteen miles to Cumberland Gap.

Tender: having the weakness or delicacy of youth; immature.
Unable or unaccustomed to endure hardship, fatigue, etc.;
delicately reared; effeminate (*sic*). Of animals or plants:
delicate, easily injured by severe weather or unfavorable conditions;
needing protection. In reference to color

or light: of a fine or delicate quality or nature; soft; subdued.
Of things immaterial, subjects, topics: easy to injure
by tactless treatment; needing cautious or delicate handling.

Peel back the eyegrain to discover the perpetrator,
the last image beheld by the victim. What darker declivity.

❖

Tenderloin, tendinous, tenderfoot. It gets cold
inside the castle at night, even in summer. We light fires in the grates.
Where did the other men go, the river is singing.

If you are magic you can heal me, Alice Notley writes.
We could make blame a pretty song, as in:
Who started this bleeding? We could weave a tune around it,
teach the tune to children. Create a folk tradition.
That is, assuming we want to heal,
stop the bleeding. We have to want to stop the bleeding.
The taste so sweet I couldn't tell that I was bleeding.
And then, when I saw the blood, I thought it was just some new,
unexpected sweetness. Strawberry liqueur, perhaps.

For a moment I took pleasure in swallowing my own blood.

Tender: 1666, an offer made in writing by one party
(frequently to a public body) to execute,
at an inclusive price or uniform rate, an order for the supply
or purchase of goods, or for the execution of work
the details of which have been submitted by another party.

The body complete within its wound. The body complete,
unpierced, unshielded. All the ghosts are wearing spectacles.
Is that some new thing you're doing with your hair.

❖

The dream of flight is the dream of *Noli me tangere*,
to be shown the separable soul. Nobody ever asks whether Icarus
had any good reason to get *away* from his father.
Or from anyone else, for that matter.
It's assumed altitude was its own reward, or light.

Because it's a myth, we are not talking about a dead *person* here.
We can perform the autopsy in language and not feel
anything. Right? (You're out of the room, somewhere else;
I can hear you humming, maybe in the kitchen.)

The thing is, it's hard not to care, with our bodies
covered in vibrating ashes, and all the patterns these ashes make.

The thing is, they are only patterns if we see them, and as such.

❖

War makes us more literate in the language of the body,
that is, the language of scars. Knowledge increases.
We talked about it, and what we were hearing on the radio, it all
seemed more or less like what we'd heard before
which made it, if not OK, then ambient, part of the same dream.

And oh! the little boats in the harbor, how we love them,
how the painters love them, perched at the pier, on the quay,
plein air. Tender: 1675, a smaller vessel commissioned
to attend men-of-war, chiefly for supplying them with stores,
conveying intelligence, dispatches, etc. 1853, a small steamer
used to carry passengers, luggage, mail, goods, etc.
to or from a larger vessel. 1825, a carriage specially constructed
to carry fuel and water for a locomotive engine, to the rear
of which it is attached. (Accompanying photograph.)

Carpal tunnel, little war in the wrist, little hollow script.
I saw this morning morning's minion, dapple-dawn-drawn
falcon / boy / falcon / woman / kestrel / language / boy.

We flense the corpse, cut the skin in strips, feed them
through the projector. Please accept this gold-plated rib
on behalf of the city, as a token of the city's esteem.

❖

As for Dolly, someone cloned her, and then someone—
the same someone, or someone else, working for the same
someone—bred her (to a Welsh mountain ram,
says Wikipedia). She gave birth three times, in 1998
to a single lamb, in 1999 to twins, in 1999 to triplets.
Bonnie, Sally, Rosie, Lucy, Darcy, Cotton.
In 2003 she died of *Jaagsiekte*, a lung disease
caused by the retrovirus JSRN, common enough
among sheep. Her cloned genetic material may
or may not have contributed to her abbreviated lifespan.

Within sight of Pictish cupmarks, their standing stones.

War comes, and is partly archaeological.
We are excavating our bodies from our bodies,
away from other bodies. Light plays a role: brush away
the soil, the enclitic grammar of the flesh.

❖

A philatelist, a funambulist, and an off-duty toxicologist
walk into a bar. Does this make them a wave function
and if so at what point does the law intervene?
(Legal tender, money or other things that may legally
be offered in payment; currency prescribed by law.)

Dear Brigham Young,
I can't make my Ann Lee doll talk anymore.
Lower lives demand more ghosts,
lightning's (other) electoral college.

I still think story is the more generous gift
though it fails and, in failing, drives
whole economies towards consolation.

At rest, looking out of the frame of the photograph.

❖

Pollen settles on the dig, the camp, the bomb site.
Children gather it carefully, take it to the assay office
where they're told (a) it's worthless and (b)
they are all now starring in their own capitalist fable.

Shower of gold, the Greeks said, when a god
entered a body. Sometimes figured in medieval paintings
as light, sometimes as hard currency.

You lie on your stomach and the gun goes off
somewhere: in Iraq, in Uruguay. At Gettysburg.
In the next apartment, where the old lady
with all the cats lives. You don't have to hear it.

A bit of broiled fish, to prove that one is not a ghost.
Enucleated, by touch we sing what's beautiful
must be an action, something you can do with your hands.

Gender asks, what is it you're to do with your hands.

PART V
THE CHERRY-TREE SINGING

The earth, entrusted with its own
heavy body, rather than, say, one single, immense
sheet of diamond or glass. Things pull and push
in their own registers, that is, into themselves.
Our own blithe gravities, green—
or green and brown—acceding in their turn.

The quality of the interruptions we make
in light: plowman, cardsharp, pedestrian. In the dark
spaces gender doesn't go, the accoutrements.

Two currencies at hand. I thread them both
into the projector. Someone else will have to switch it
on. What Brakhage would have done, texture
to the mind's eye's thought: rootbark, cornhusk.

It is not a question of reviving the old songs,
the greenwood of intention,
of the inner ear: one leaf falls, settles, rises again.

First person, second person, third.
Murders multiply, each a little sanctioned
by light's imperial tribunal. Pretty pictures, the blood
in its canoes of silk and wax, the living semblances
light hangs from faith, history's taut line.

A flicker in time's breeze, male and female.
We recognize ourselves, and—something else. What?

❖

The argument that art effects empathy expired
at Auschwitz, if not Austerlitz. Still, that bleeding of mind

into mind, and outside time. Review: to look again
into well, into dovecote, the castle's deepest places.
Once upon a time we all lived in the castle,
thinks the Irish novelist, tiptoeing down the master
stair for a glass of sherry before dinner.
As if we had just set foot on this island
for the first time, and been greeted by our better selves.

Citizens, almost by right of birth; integers
in some math loneliness is polishing
until they're sharp: we're going
to be late for our rendezvous with the nation-state.
The God in whose presence our absence
percolates, cavitates, lets go of every string.
All those bodies, kites, islands
oxidant, kindled as with fire. Your heart
among them, beating time. This invisible music.

Inside the created lies the uncreated. Outside, also.

❖

Asylum, then. From the macroverse
of shapes and forms, the interlocking faiths
our bodies make. From metaphor's preemptive
madeleine and, further, exilic, a Gilead
for wanderlust, assumptive introspection.

It rained and, from our berths in steerage,
from our seats above the damaged wing we felt
that slight, expulsive rocking.
(The nation-states put out their APBs.)
Catchment for silence and what was
silence, the city. We are the city. We were
the castle and its mirrored shards.
Peel back the eyegrain, the bruised heel.

A glass of wine on your name-day
when we know it, and adding to that benison.
All the animals in the photograph look kind,
don't you think?   —Don't you want them to?

Can gender be a lyric form?
Matins ritual of green and blue. Tomorrow
the recyclers come. How neighborly
the midges and bromides, the ladywalk at dusk.
How neighborly, this resurrection.

❖

Bypath, moss-clocked (I almost wrote
-Glocked), overledged with rills that look,
you insisted, *laid*, as if by human hands. A stone
bridge suggests a venerable
interval of use, of vectored preference.

A river makes use of pronouns. Something
haunts the body that is not the body.
Call it river, if you like. Gender too, if you like.

The stile, which had been open wide,
unlatched every other time I passed, latched fast
on this particular afternoon.
I unlatch it, step through, think to latch it back
and decide not to, since I plan to return
quite soon, the way I came. When I return
(the way I came) it's latched again.

We make paintings and call them "eternal life"
because we know color persists
beyond memory. We see the same colors
the dead see (though they may in fact see more).

Bumblebees, yes, but no honeybees
among the raspberries, the blackberry blossoms,
the woundwort and rosebay willowherb.
Somehow we survived all that,
the hive mind, representational language
as such. We had not, perhaps, planned to be here.

Points of connection: (I) water, and
(2) we see the same colors the dead still see.

❖

In the painting called *Eternal Life*,
dumpsters overflowing with trash behind
the Beeslack projects.
The problem is, we don't really know things
until we know them in language.

Today at Firth viaduct, someone—two different
someones, actually—has left flowers
tucked into the chain-link. One bears a note
to "David," hoping he will "rest in peace."

The horses in the fields below all wear
thick navy horse blankets, though it's not cold.
They look more creaturely this way.

I pass beneath another bridge and think
I could live here. We could, we think, live
anywhere, almost anywhere,
translucent, precatory. The appeal to desire,
quiver in the fernbank, the blowzy
rhododendron: we watch, we want to make
something *of* it, that vergency, that rustling.

❖

Things speak another language and you
want to shake them the way you might shake
a disobedient child, a rug, a politician
in some fantasy of communication
or revenge. You want to shake them until
something falls out: a dime, a lost earring, the cap
to your favorite fountain pen. A brass key,
a passport. You want to keep shaking.

Because it's what the dead want,
what we want to do with our terrible dead.

Maybe they're shaking us, and something
falls out, we see it, pick it up, hold it
up to the radiant light, it shines, we're puzzled,
I'm handing it to you now, look at this,
what do you think it could have been?

All rivers were once fallen trees,
writes Alice Oswald. I want to believe this
because it makes a pretty picture in my mind.

Eternal life, pretty picture in the mind.

❖

In Mauricewood, three miles away,
sixty-three men and boys were entombed in 1889
by a mine fire. The funeral cortège
(after some of the bodies were recovered)
was organized by religious affiliation:
Presbyterian, Anglican, Roman Catholic.
The rest of the bodies were recovered, and
presumably buried, six months later,
without reference to profession or creed.

It hurts, whined the smaller of two boys on the path.
It hurts, mimicked his older brother.
Why don't you just go home to your mummy

in this season of yarrow and hawkweed.
I wanted to add, with the foxglove just ending
and the heath orchids starting to sputter,
to burn out, one by one, stars
that didn't quite know they were stars,
were unclear on the concept, as the comedians
put it—were testing their own small
gravities, just getting things off the ground—

The smaller of the two boys has started to snivel.
His older brother kicks him in the shin
once, smartly, and then turns, as if to walk on alone.

Which one of them do you want to shake more?

❖

Asylum, then: antiphonal. Likenesses
just out of phase: tree limb, nightbird, a song
that crosses itself, intersects.
And we want to live there, we want
this marriage, that stallion, this firmament.

Scaffold of river, the moral imagination
a liquid place, terra infirma.
Appositional to appetite, these monuments
to weight, to weight's measure: approach
and, as from mercy—or from mercy's god—
render. Heartbeat. Currency.
Carol pawned from sleep and then, sleep-
wasted, apse-castored, a little spare change.
In the shape of a five-pointed star.
In the shape of a six-pointed star, which is,

as any child discovers, nothing
but two triangles,
superimposed. A doodle, a longer night.

In the next room, sleepers brush the bruised
hands of intent from their sleeping selves.
A safe place, slab of secretary
where worlds huddle, insensate to mythology.
Or, better: words blind them, mirrors
that reflect the eye back on itself
so that shadows, those other pedigrees,
don't startle. Asylum: soothing in its octaves,
its canny mimesis of breath and register.

Song, then: to rouse the sleepers, to alert
the angel to your presence.
Like most births, this is easier underwater.

❖

The angel studies the problem,
angle of incident vs. angle of reflection.
You want to help him, only
he's so much bigger than you are, and on fire.

The pronouns cluster thickly at the mouth
of the forge, each a flayed skin beating time
against another flayed skin, perforated
where the projector did its clumsy work.

Language wades into its needlework, calf-
deep, thigh-deep. Skin to skin, pelt to pelfry.
It is a white wedding and everyone's invited,
only you're late, or misdirected—
went to the wrong chapel, the wrong
garden apartment—stuck in traffic. Or maybe
you never received the invitation.

The projector tears open its own throat-beam
of light and expects everything else—
all matter—to do likewise. Something issues,
as from that infundibulum which is not
light, neither image nor image's circumstance.

You watch, as from a distance, blinded.
Something in your body remembers. You are
not frightened, though you should be.

❖

It's dawn again now, the early dawn
of the northernmost latitudes in summer.
The raptors are confused.
The light feels all wrong, global,
a bypass for the city's choking breath.

Treble descant, the rosebank
by the kennel obscuring sound and smell.
This is not a creation story.
The dogs in their cages bark almost
incessantly, but not quite.

Watching the old moon, you paged
your way through a dusty magazine
without reading anything,
really without even glancing down
at the glossy photos. You said,
It's light enough to read by.
You wanted to be able to say that.

Or maybe we're bored with angels.
Maybe the angel's other name is gender
and we've been soaking in it, all along.
Hawkweed, yarrow, bloodwort.
Prick of pulse at the wrist. Light calling.

One could do worse than believe:
in premise, conclusion,
in the lurid patterning of artifact.

Into the fire go the pronouns and their
hollow, heavy jewelry. They seem
to want this, we tell ourselves, glistening
in the light of the soiled lithograph.

❖

Dear Alice Oswald, I keep misreading
the titles of your poems. You wrote
"Three Portraits of a Radio Audience,"
but this morning, shocked from sleep
by what I think might be high
blood pressure from last night's steak-
and-kidney pie, I read
"Three Portraits of a Radio *Ambulance.*"

As hook, as map, intermittently pulsing,
with heat or breath or livid circulation,
you can't say with any certainty.

For twenty years I believed men and women
could be friends outside of marriage.
It was a book I carried with me,
to the market, to the post office.
It was—I did not know it—a book on fire,
a text concealed inside a stress fracture.

A different river, a different
lay-by, by-blow of some different
season/era/orogeny/epoch.
Begets floods begets fields
and factories, dimity and rag-bond in their turn.
Sleep worked here. Sleep lives here.

When I asked what it was the former
inhabitants did in the caves, our guide said,
"Live in them." Then she shrugged.

An army of bloodless tongues
gathered on the plain: call this *distance.*

❖

It is possible to train one's voice
in imitation of a nightbird, a raptor,
assorted gullible waterfowl, even the deer
in their rutting chuff and bark.

Completion nods, absorbed in
something else, Myanmar or Paraguay.
Attention and its consort, the posture
of attention: *pay,* idiom insists
and it's not wrong. The question, then:
to what extent is gender a posture
of attention, and in this guise a form?

The body paying attention to other
bodies, to differences between bodies
in spite of what I wanted, a writing
around the body, as with light,
a history lesson color was to teach.

Dot, dash, the Picts and their cupping stones.
What enters the body legitimately
now a question for the Naval Academy,
the Supreme Court, a trial of metals,
coin, bullion by touch, fire, etc.
Or: to adjudicate weights, measure,
the quality of bread by legal standards.

What does the glove say, sign language
in search of its interpreter inside
its pit of spit and crude bone splinter?

❖

Even you, in my idea of you, bent low
over this plate/diaphragm/membrane
where ashes collect. Personification
is a perfectly venerable literary enterprise
(see: the gods [as vectors for]).
But this is not a play, as you maintain.

When I was a child, everybody
turned out to watch the river rise
through the old downtown, warehouses
and disused stemming sheds, then red-
brick stores nobody I knew
patronized, and then,
further up, if the rain continued,
the shoe shop and the jeweler's,
the old-time pharmacy with its bar
stools and phosphates, the button mill, last
the highways leading out of town
south, east, and west.
We brought folding chairs for this
and complained about the Corps
of Engineers, who were supposed to fix
the problem. Everything they tried
only made it worse.
Eventually, we paid them off to go away
and the floods stopped, as if by magic.

Maybe the gods grew bored. Maybe
the river succumbed to television,
sits watching now on some immense set
the same images that transfix us.

Image, and the idea of image, ideas
that swim behind image, in the eddies,
nanometer wavelength baptisms.

Someone has to play the role
of the innocent, star in the photograph,
plan Roman roads and Easter lunches.
There was an island, but we mistook it
for a sailboat. We're still
inside it, waiting for a proper wind.

Perfect attention. The waters rise
and so we try some other voices
out, tongue-in-glove, hooked, secure.

❖

The city grows around us. One day
we see, in a much-praised museum show,
a painting of some policemen,
and then, before we know it,
we're there inside that photograph
wearing someone else's clothes.

The nation state confirms the body's
title to—not much, it seems.
What it protects it soon incorporates,
Dolly and the deer; the castle and the chapel,
novels, raptors in their turn. Only then,
by looking up, can we see the acrobats
descending on thin, blackened wires.

To ventriloquize without the aid
of personification, without personifying
at least from your point of view.
It's the intelligence, or else
the moral imagination come calling

as a figure of the mind, electric
ditto-graph of neural pathways
lighting up one hemisphere or
the other. I forget how this part goes
but never mind, attend the figures

cliché now stains with wax
to keep them smoother, brighter,
improve their durability. Here, try one.
It's—almost—as if they're free.

❖

Full stop, digestion and its discontents.
Symbolic logic abuses a thrush
in the vicinity of the outsourced
nuclear reactor and we call this something
to do on hot days, in the shade.

Precordial, what lies in front
of the heart: breastbone, ribcage,
sinew. Latin making such a pretty logic,
antecordial: what lies behind the heart.
Spinal cord, shoulder blade.

The point is, the body cleaves
and in planes, anaclastic. Springs back
with a crackling sound (now rare).

When I had cancer, they cut me open
once, twice, three times,
not counting the venipuncture.
Other things happened too.
Sometimes I was conscious, but
never enough to read. Reading
required too much effort.
I let legend wash over my body

like some new color everyone
was talking about on their way
to the movies, something important
but not too important, not yet.

It's not that I was bored. Boredom
requires something of the body,
something of the embodied mind—

During that time people who loved me
moved through me like ghosts.

We hoist the ensign of our deliverer
into the firmament above the castle,
not really expecting anything
other than, perhaps, rain. —It rains.

❖

Corrosive slit, soloist in the sonogram,
the body blots gyreward, gust of protein
consolation hasn't yet wiped
from the etched flank of this glass slide.

Aurora dentata. Light with teeth.

Sometimes, the body offers pain up
to the night and we don't know
whether we're growing or dying,
starting to grow or starting to die.
You could get up, drink a glass of water,
play a piece or two on the organ—
if you have an organ, if the pieces
are relatively short. You could
turn on a light, read a few pages
of a book. You could watch a movie
or put on some clothes, take a walk

outside, just for walking or, further yet,
to the all-night bodega, for nachos.

All dolls are deer dolls completion
dandles inside a necklace the city
wears, its graceful catenary
like a lone swimmer in an otherwise
deserted stretch of virgin surf, arm arched
above the current, in moonlight.

In this photograph, you can just make out
the swimmer, in the middle distance.
He doesn't look any smaller
than we do, only, well, perhaps a little
more labile, a little more resilient.
In the photograph, you can't
tell what he's swimming towards,
if anything. He's swimming away from you.

❖

Sleep advertises a famous resurrection
love has been sharing with the other animals
in a clearing somewhere in the forest.
You're fighting your way towards this place
with the only weapon gender has given
you, a rib you've sharpened
to a crescent, a scimitar, a graceful husk.

Ruthless fathers and sons hack away
at the undergrowth you've commandeered,
much to the delight of the audience
back in the city. (They're watching on CCTV.)
The angel of the state produces
a skeleton key, complete with antioxidants.
Everyone dives for it, even the ghosts,
Iphigenia, Icarus propped in his sunshroud.

SpellCheck is still not convinced Icarus
exists, that he ever existed.
Technology's doubts are the wounds in Icarus's
blue feet, his pale, unclouded shins.

You don't have to wear much
when you're a ghost. You've nothing to hide
and besides, it doesn't get colder there, only
History won't let you take your shoes
to Goodwill. The dead wish they could be
more useful than they generally are.

❖

There's blood on the wall, you say, I dreamt
there was blood on a low stone wall.
Were there children in the dream, I ask,
without looking up from my book.
A few minutes pass. You're behind me,
in the bathroom I think, I can't see
what you're doing. —Maybe, you say, at last.

The river doesn't take sides, is one fact,
and neither do photographs, is another.
Vagile (adj.)—*chiefly bot.*—endowed with
or having freedom of movement,
able to move about or disperse in a given
environment, as a plant or animal species.

The mouth is a ghost, someone said,
but I let it pass, there didn't seem any point
in arguing. A posigrade rocket
is one fired in the precise direction
of its target, rather than at some higher mark.

Therefore, the river is a photograph?
That light was taking, and we got in the way?

❖

Thus, full circle—husk—flayed skins
of the instrumentalists from their bondage,
the soloist in the hospital blotting out
every dark stone in the citadel,
every code-bearing enigma in the chapel.
Everyone: forked accident, in tourist class.

It changes everything when deep down
you think something has an end.
The eschatology of our condition:
the trumpets, the trial, all clues brought
properly to bear at the wedding feast.

Completion dries grass against
an abandoned wire fence
carefully, almost tenderly, blade by blade.
One plus one plus one plus one,
ictus, downbeat, ordinal pulse.

One plus one plus one plus one plus one.
Fragment of ensign, of citadel.
I hoist this flag above the hospital
where gender keeps turning the pages
of a glossy magazine, looking at the photos.
The photos are poems, you understand—
it's that kind of dream—
but gender's not allowed to read them.

❖

There was a map with a ghost in it
and we held it in our hands, while we danced.
The police stood by and watched.
Some of the policemen were paintings.
God's rib, twinkling above the city,
like Icarus refusing to fall, or not entirely.

Asylum: this is not that sort of book.
Asylum: quest for a lyric form
that organizes, recognizes, that completes:
light and ministry, wood and edifice, faith and
poison, the ambitions of children.

Step into the body and the dress
the body wears, little buckle-glimpses,
rogue claimant under martial law.
Asylum: to have stopped believing
in the advertising, the labyrinth's
pericarp, bituminous. Asylum: we live
in the labyrinth, and its dependencies.

ALL VISITORS MUST REPORT
TO RECEPTION, the sign still blazoned
just beyond the razed paper mill.
I misread yet again, in a book by a friend:
"Surveillance is the elsewhere of God."

Still, the pageant needs more music,
capitalism says, more *Geldwelt,* more love.

Six times, seven times, the Pakistani
sprinter. It's getting light now, in the east.

The moral imagination says, Come home.

NOTE(S)

Testament originated as an exploration of and response to three texts: *Lisa Robertson's Magenta Soul Whip* (Coach House Press, 2009); Carla Harryman, *Adorno's Noise* (Essay Press, 2008); and Alice Notley, *Alma, or The Dead Women* (Granary Books, 2006). What could have been a book review or critical essay evolved into a long poem, in keeping perhaps with John Taggart's suggestion that criticism of a genre should take place within that genre. Subsequent waves of revision have moved the poem away from some of its original gestures and closer to others.

Many thanks to these poets for their sustaining work (and to Alice Oswald and others I was reading at the same time, as per references below). Gratitude to the Hawthornden International Retreat for Writers, where this poem was drafted over twelve days in July 2009, and to Yaddo and the Virginia Center for the Creative Arts, where it was revised in November 2009 and May 2012. Thanks to Dan Poppick for being an early reader of the manuscript, and to Peter Conners. Portions of *Testament* appeared previously in the journals *New Orleans Review, Berkeley Poetry Review, Modern Language Studies, The Journal, Court Green, Hotel Amerika, Fourteen Hills, Seattle Review, Interim,* and *Bat City Review,* to the editors of which I am also grateful.

REFERENCES

The title of Part I is derived from these lines by Lisa Robertson: ". . . The / Symptom takes on the historical / Function of a hero, who may purchase / For himself a plasticity imagined / As geography because it is / Visible. . . ." (from "Coda: The Device," in *Lisa Robertson's Magenta Soul Whip,* 86).

11   *digestive and genital organs of plants*   from J. R. R. Tolkien's short story "Leaf by Niggle" (although for years I somehow misattributed the phrase to Aldous Huxley).

14   *A bridal texture*   See *Lisa Robertson's Magenta Soul Whip,* 51 ("a bridal textile").

26   *A mannerist ecology*   *Lisa Robertson's Magenta Soul Whip,* 64.

34   *sensual communication*   Harryman, *Adorno's Noise,* 13.

35   Blanchot quote is from Maurice Blanchot, *The Writing of the Disaster,* translated by Ann Smock (University of Nebraska Press, 1986), 23.

41   *I want to see the policemen / in their white masks. . . . / In the Mardi Gras parade.*   Paweł

Wojtasik's video and sound installation *Below Sea Level* (2009).

Here are the sirens of not knowing / everything Harryman, *Adorno's Noise*, 40.

45 *Have you discussed this with your mother* See Harryman, *Adorno's Noise*, 84 ("I have discussed this with my mother....," along with Harryman's own flag-raising/-lowering anxieties).

47 *concept vs. need* See Lisa Robertson's *Magenta Soul Whip*, 11 ("for you are shadow and concept with no memory no vestige no need").

51 *This can be a little unnerving* See Harryman, *Adorno's Noise*, 123.

Writing, without placing itself . . . Blanchot, *The Writing of the Disaster*, 53; Levinas quote is *idem*, 77.

52 *Something large and real / and beyond all sacrifice* Misquotation of Harryman, *Adorno's Noise*, 128 ("something large and real beyond all artifice").

53 *The body wants to be art and fails at it* Harryman, *Adorno's Noise*, 144.

55 *the room in which one lives / anticipates one's burial in a Christian plot* Harryman, *Adorno's Noise*, 17.

59 *If you surround yourself with the dead / then you worship the dead* In response to "Rite to Divest Oneself of the Need to Worship," in Notley, *Alma*, 323.

60 *If writing, then, is "thought's patience"* See Blanchot, *The Writing of the Disaster*, 41.

66 *Follow your discomfort* Notley, *Alma*, 21.

74 *The matrilineal power of self- / obsession, I misread"* and *Another misreading: God's / viscous omniscience* Notley, *Alma*, 46 ("we had a matrilineal power of self-possession before the europeans came" and "God's vicious omniscience," respectively).

75 *we are not safe* In response to "Safe Owl," in Notley, *Alma*, 50.

79 *Outside. Neutral. Disaster. Return.* Blanchot, *The Writing of the Disaster*, 57–58.

88 *beautiful country burn again* From Robinson Jeffers's poem "Apology for Bad Dreams" via Joan Didion, *After Henry* (Vintage, 1993), 217.

You will take a new name from a man / if you privilege the antiquity of his song In response to "The Snake," in Notley, *Alma*, 147.

93 *A symbol / which interests us* also */ as an object is distracting* Susanne Langer as quoted by Rosmarie Waldrop in "Alarms and Excursions," in Charles Bernstein, ed., *The Politics of Poetic Form* (Roof, 1990), 60.

Harryman quote from her poem "Sites," in *Under the Bridge* (This Press, 1980), 29.

Zucker quote from Rachel Zucker, *The Last Clear Narrative* (Wesleyan, 2004), 100.

95 *The familiar Mercator projection . . . latitudes.* From the 1974 edition of *The Encyclopedia Britannica*, vol. 11, p. 476, under "Maps and Mapping."

96 *And—yes—Lilith / we have met | and do I know you?* Geoffrey Hill, *Speech! Speech!* (Counterpoint, 2000), 4.

97 Nephite references from Ernest W. Baughman, *Type and Motif Index of the Folktales of England and North America* (Bloomington: Indiana University Folklore Series, 1966), 392–393.

99 *Sky Burial, my friend is thinking / of entitling her new manuscript, / now that the Palestinians / have the right to choose.* *Sky Burial* by Dana Levin (Copper Canyon, 2011); see also

Notley, *Alma*, 193.

101 *human eyes / or humanlike*   Notley, *Alma*, 196.

102 The Antoine Volodine novel is *Minor Angels*, translated by Jordan Stump (University of Nebraska Press, 2004).
enemy aircraft / installation   Notley, *Alma*, 198.

103 "Mr. Bojangles" and "Put Your Hands inside the Puppet Head" are songs by Jerry Jeff Walker and They Might Be Giants, respectively.
New studies suggest my conducting teacher / was wrong: memory holds seven (+/- three) things at a time.   See Mark Cunningham, *Body Language* (Tarpaulin Sky, 2008), 54.

104 *chestnut geldings on the beach*   From John McPhee's "The Search for Marvin Gardens" (in John D'Agata, ed., *The Next American Essay* [Graywolf, 2003], 19).

115 *They're men, she said, I couldn't / even take them to a cosmetics counter.*   Singer Chrissie Hynde, quoted in *The Scotsman*, 12 July 2009.

119 *because an image tells it to?*   See Notley, *Alma*, 309.

122 *darker declivity*   Notley, *Alma*, 313.
If you are magic you can heal me   Notley, *Alma*, 315.

131 *All rivers were once fallen trees, / writes Alice Oswald*   In *Dart* (Faber & Faber, 2002), 12.

135 *Three Portraits of a Radio Audience*   In Alice Oswald, *Woods Etc.* (Faber & Faber, 2005), 36.

136 *What enters the body legitimately*   Cunningham, *Body Language*, 13.

137 *But this is not a play, as you maintain*   Alice Oswald, *A Sleepwalk on the Severn* (Faber & Faber, 2009), 1.

112 *Surveillance is the elsewhere of God*   Misreading of Simon Smith, *Mercury* (Salt Publishing, 2006), 26 ("Surveillance in the absence of God").

Other references, in passing: Ernst Chladni, Neda Soltan, Dolly, Ann Lee, the OED, Joseph Cornell.

About the Author

G.C. Waldrep's most recent books are *Your Father on the Train of Ghosts* (BOA Editions, 2011), a collaboration with John Gallaher; *The Arcadia Project: North American Postmodern Pastoral* (Ahsahta, 2012), co-edited with Joshua Corey; and a chapbook, *Susquehanna* (Omnidawn, 2013). Waldrep's work has appeared in *Poetry, Ploughshares, APR, New England Review, New American Writing, Harper's, Tin House, Verse,* and many other journals, as well as in *Best American Poetry 2010* and the second edition of Norton's *Postmodern American Poetry.* He has received prizes from the Poetry Society of America and the Academy of American Poets, as well as the Colorado Prize, the Dorset Prize, the Campbell Corner Prize, two Pushcart Prizes, a Gertrude Stein Award for Innovative American Writing, and a 2007 National Endowment for the Arts Fellowship in Literature. Waldrep lives in Lewisburg, Pennsylvania, where he teaches at Bucknell University, is Editor for the literary journal *West Branch,* and serves as Editor-at-Large for *The Kenyon Review.*

BOA Editions, Ltd.
American Poets Continuum Series

Colophon

BOA Editions, Ltd., a not-for-profit publisher of poetry and other literary works, fosters readership and appreciation of contemporary literature. By identifying, cultivating, and publishing both new and established poets and selecting authors of unique literary talent, BOA brings high-quality literature to the public. Support for this effort comes from the sale of its publications, grant funding, and private donations.

The publication of this book is made possible, in part,
by the special support of the following individuals:

Anonymous x 2
Armbruster Family Foundation
Piotr & Dena Florczyk
Michael Hall
Melissa Hall & Joe Torre
Chandra V. McKenzie
Boo Poulin
Deborah Ronnen & Sherman Levey
Steven O. Russell & Phyllis Rifkin-Russell
Gerald Vorrasi